Nick Davies

HOW TO BE
GREAT
AT THE STUFF
YOU HATE

The
Straight Talking
Guide to Persuading,
Networking and Selling

HOW TO
BE GREAT AT
THE STUFF
YOU HATE

The Straight-Talking Guide to Networking, Persuading and Selling

Nick Davies

CAPSTONE

This edition first published 2012
© 2012 Nick Davies

Registered office
Capstone Publishing Ltd. (A Wiley Company), The Atrium, Southern Gate,
Chichester, West Sussex, PO19 8SQ United Kingdom

For details of our global editorial offices, for customer services and for information
about how to apply for permission to reuse the copyright material in this book
please see our website at www.wiley.com.

Library of Congress Cataloguing-in-Publication Data

9780857082435 (paperback), ISBN 9780857082565 (ebk),
ISBN 9780857082572 (ebk), ISBN 9780857082589 (ebk)

A catalogue record for this book is available from the British Library.

Set in 10 on 13.5 pt Adobe Caslon Pro by Toppan Best-set Premedia Limited
Printed in Great Britain by TJ International Ltd.

This book is for George and Harry: my sons.

You make me laugh, cry, shout, become exasperated, glow with pride, but most of all you show me what life is really all about.

How you choose to earn your living, boys, is up to you, just do something you enjoy: life's too short.

I dedicate this book to you both. You'll only know how much I love you when you are fathers yourselves one day.

Dad

CONTENTS

FOREWORD

HOW TO BE GREAT AT THE STUFF YOU HATE

Nick Davies and I have four things in common:

- we both started our working lives in the school of hard knocks (he sold shoes, I sold soft drinks)
- we share a penchant for expensive shoes
- we like lawyers
- and we both now sell services

True, you may never have heard of me and yes, true again, I *am* a mate of Nick's. But who cares? Because this book is about you. It's about seizing the power of the good old-fashioned common sense most of you were born with, but have since unlearned.

As breaths of fresh air go, Nick's book goes furthest. I have been selling for a third of a century and found it un-put-down-able. Even though it can be read in one sitting with ease, it is equally designed for "grazing" in spare moments – on a plane or on a train.

Where to start? Where better than the role of selling in our lives? Right up front we are reminded of a fundamental truth:

Sales = Tax = Civilised Society

Let's work backwards on that. A civilised, capitalist society cannot function without public services. Public services can't function without the "tax-dollar". And taxes wouldn't exist without someone somewhere selling something.

Then there's the structure of the book. It is one of its many merits. The process – no the *art* – of selling is broken down forensically into simple, practical steps. Steps which remind us how easy selling can be if only we follow common sense.

Nick is generous with his tips too, using humour, anecdote and example to bring them to life. The hard part, he says, is perseverance – having the dogged determination, self-confidence and optimism to keep going when others fade.

Nick has an inimitable style: chatty, engaging, amusing, pacey. And this is the real secret of the book's success. It's like a friendly, encouraging coach in your ear.

Gold-dust is sprinkled liberally throughout. You will discover that you should – indeed *must* – fall back in love with the phone. You'll be shown the value of small-talk when networking. You will be given clear ground-rules covering when – and when not – to kiss! You will realise the importance of following up on meetings. You will find out how asking for business compares with courtship. And, finally, you'll come face to face with the thing we fear most, silence, and the knack of knowing when to zip the lip.

Most crucially, we are reminded why we have twice as many ears as we have a mouth. And we find that the best listeners make the best sales people. To that end, whilst the book is already graced with nine useful quotations, I'd like to add a 10th:

"Knowledge speaks, but wisdom listens." (Jimi Hendrix)

If selling is about making it easy for people to buy, with this book Nick Davies makes it a whole lot easier for you to make it easy for people to buy from *you*.

Simon Slater – Managing Director, Intelligent Office Consulting Services Limited.

INTRODUCTION

'You cannot bore people into buying from you.'

David Ogilvy, founder of Ogilvy & Mather,
one of the largest ad agencies in the world.

About This Book

This book is about selling and developing business – which, if we're honest, a lot of people hate. In truth, it's not that they hate it; rather, they dislike the idea of doing something they associate with lots of particularly negative characteristics.

That is peculiar, since all of us are selling all of the time.

If you've ever persuaded your mates to go for a curry rather than a Chinese, or cajoled your missus into watching *We Came, We Saw, We Shot Them All to Pieces* when she'd suggested *Mr D'Arcy and His Romantic Loveliness*, or you've persuaded your boss that you should have next Tuesday off, then you, my friend, have been selling – it's just that you weren't aware that was what you were doing.

We are attempting to influence people all the time: at work, at home, friends, relatives, colleagues (co-workers, if you're American). We persuade them of our ideas, suggestions, compromises, offers, plans, strategy and even 'us'. When you fire off a CV or sit in an interview, you are selling yourself – literally: 'Choose me instead of the other 10 on your short list.'

And yet, when 'selling' becomes part of someone's job description or an imperative because they've opted to start their own business, they suddenly get all panicky about it. Rather than approach it instinctively, as they have been doing in their everyday dealings with people, they begin looking at it from a kind of intellectual, almost academic viewpoint, and thus become terribly awkward, 'clunky' and gauche about the whole thing.

Well, stop it!

Selling is common sense, creativity and personality, not science and certainly not of the rocket variety. (Having said that, a criminal psychologist I met recently, who has a friend who's an actual rocket scientist, told me that she'd been told by said friend that there's not that much to rocket science anyway – so there!)

When people are asked to find words or phrases that best describe sales people and sales reps, they come up with some or all of the following: pushy, uncaring, slimy, smooth (not in a good way), hard-faced, 'make people buy things they don't want', 'don't listen to what you want but sell what they want you to have', 'are only interested in the money', 'don't care what they sell as long as they hit their target', 'will tell you anything to get a sale', 'use underhand tricks and tactics to bamboozle people'. You get the point.

However, the truth is that those who excel at selling and developing business are none of those things. In fact, if you come across anyone exhibiting these traits you're dealing with an amateur – really good sales people behave differently.

About Me

I have been selling since 1983. Over that time I've run four businesses, which I started from scratch.

This book is down to earth and practical. It is based on what I have learned over the years, some of it in a classroom or from a book, but 99% of it by actually doing it – by making huge cock-ups, losing big deals, losing my house and nearly going bankrupt, but also making some money along the way.

This book is opinionated. You'll agree with some of it and you'll hate other bits. Hey, I can live with that – as long as you get something out of it.

This book is also personal. What follows is written from my point of view, based on my experiences. Other sales people will have had similar experiences, but not the same. The book is full of stories and anecdotes – my stories and anecdotes, things I have done, written, said and experienced.

There's a lot of stuff about winning business in the professional services sector, in particular the legal profession. That's because I sell training and coaching services and most of my work is with lawyers (I used to be one and I like them).

That said, what you'll read here is as applicable to selling products or other services. I've sold shoes, sandwiches, handbags, storecards, phone systems, leasing and rental agreements for office products, radio airtime and people (I was a director of a recruitment firm, not a people trafficker), so I know about selling products too.

This is just one book about selling: it's not intended to be the definitive guide. There are loads of other books out there, so go and read them too – but understand this: the only way you'll actually get good at selling is by doing rather than reading. You can read about how to swim, but if you don't get in the pool then what's the point?

Who Should Read This Book?

Anyone can read this book, but it's mainly intended for those who are not sales people but find themselves having to develop business as part of their role, like a lawyer, accountant, senior civil servant, architect, actuary or manager.

If you've started your own business or you're thinking about taking the plunge into self-employment, this book is for you too. Perhaps you make great coffee or wickedly delectable buns, or maybe you are a mechanic or printer or graphic artist or fashion designer or film producer and, while you are confident in your end product, you haven't got a clue how to go about selling what you offer.

You *can* learn this stuff. Honest!

Some people would have you believe that it takes a 'certain sort', that sales people are 'born', that you need 'the gift of the gab'. They say there are those who can and the rest can't. That's nonsense!

Selling is easy: dead easy. And once you know the basics, anyone can sell. In fact, as I've already said, you – yes, *you* – are selling all of the time.

If you are a sales rep, someone who has had structured sales training and works in a sales team, then there's material in this book that you'll like too, so read it if you want a refresher, but don't expect some kind of sales epiphany.

Why You Should Read This Book

I recommend you read this book because by the end of it you'll feel much happier about doing those things you have to do as part of your job that you just don't enjoy. You'll have become great at the stuff you hate. You'll understand how to win more work and you'll bring in more business and earn more money.

I know what I'm describing works, because people who have been on my training courses phone me and tell me. They say things like:

> *I phoned a bloke up I have really wanted to get an appointment with for ages and did some of the things you suggested and now I'm seeing him and I wanted to tell you that it really works.*

I also know it works because I do it and I earn a good living by doing it.

What's Different about This Book?

This book starts on the basis that you've found yourself doing things you never signed up to do: like network, persuade other people and sell yourself, your products or the service you offer. You're probably never going to like doing them, but what I can do is make them less painful. Once you know the tricks, you can actually be great at something even if you don't love it. Maybe by the end you will!

And here's a promise: this book contains no jargon and it gets straight to the point. Unlike most business books there will only be nine quotes and none of them are at the start of the chapters. You've had one already, but let's get another four of them out of the way right now:

> *It is only the shallow people who do not judge by appearances.*
>
> *Oscar Wilde*

> *You cannot hope to be taken seriously in poor quality shoes.*
>
> *Gore Vidal*

> *If you see a bandwagon, it's too late.*
>
> *Sir James Goldsmith*

You might feel a bit sleepy.

Dr Harold Shipman

You Don't Need to Know It All Before Getting Started

Over the past few years I have met a good number of people, both self-employed and employed, who have told me that they don't feel confident enough to go out and promote what it is they are offering without having an entire product range or detailed knowledge of everything going on in their profession.

This is silly, because in the case of the product range you'll always be able to add one more thing; and in the case of a knowledge-based service, there will always be more that you could learn!

Furthermore, what will happen if you produce a superb and comprehensive product range, only to find that when you take it to market people say: 'Well, it's great, but we'd only take it from you if you did it in blue or in a travel version.'

Surely it is far better to make a small sample, take it out to potential customers and get feedback. If enough interest is expressed in what might be a slightly amended version, then you can always produce it, but at least you haven't wasted a lot of time and money.

Product or service development is important: you cannot go to market with something that doesn't work. But equally, you only learn what customers want by going out there and talking to them. Learning on the job is what it's all about. Equally, don't think you can't sell without first knowing everything there is to know about selling: you can! Learn by your mistakes is the best way.

While I have had some structured, formal sales training, I really learnt how to sell on the job and by making horrendous mistakes and unmentionable gaffs and by losing sales.

Selling Really Is *Dead* Easy

Selling is not like performing surgery on children or constructing a pressurized water reactor, but you'd be forgiven for thinking otherwise when you look at the arrows, flow charts, schematics, pie charts, histograms and endless acronyms that lie like so much detritus across the pages of overpriced bits of nonsense about selling. If that wasn't enough, books like that also tend to carry endorsements from people you've never heard of, who are probably mates of the author anyway.

Too many non-sales people, unfamiliar with a subject that they regard as some sort of dark art, flick through these books, get the fright of their lives, and think: 'Flippin' 'eck, I knew it was complicated. My fears have been confirmed. I'll be no good at selling. Please make it all go away!'

What this book does is talk plainly about sales and developing business. After reading it you will have gained a far better understanding of what selling is, and how to go about doing it without having to remember an endless list of irritating acronyms. So let's begin by talking about selling in more detail.

CHAPTER 1

THE STUFF YOU HATE . . . SELLING

Wherever you are right now, stop, put the book down and look around. Everything you see is there because someone sold it. Everything!

The chair you are sitting on, the lights and ceiling panels above you, the desks, the coffee, the sticky bun, the cups, the air-conditioning units, your pen, your clothes, shoes, make-up, briefcase, the aircraft, bus, train or car you travelled on to get here – someone, somewhere sold it. There's a man or woman earning a living, paying their mortgage, feeding their kids, who knocked on some purchasing manager's door and persuaded them to buy that chair, that aircraft (yes, Boeing and Airbus have a sales team), that pen, those shoes, that coffee cup.

Selling is vital to our society. Organizations only make a profit if they sell something for a price greater than its cost. Out of that profit they pay corporation tax along with wages to employees, who in turn pay tax. No sales = no profit = no tax.

Doctors, nurses, teachers, firefighters and police officers don't generate profit, which means they have to be paid out of tax money – which is only generated if someone, somewhere is selling stuff. So we should be happy there are people who can sell. No one sold anything in communist countries because the state planned it all. That's why people had no money or food or medicine and were poorer than dirt.

What Is Selling?

Selling is about making it easy for people to buy. There you are: 24 years of sales experience and that's the whole lot summed up in one sentence.

I suppose you could put the book back on the shelf now and save yourself a few bob . . . But let me elaborate.

'Selling' Is a Dirty Word

At the start of my business development courses, I always ask delegates to shout out words, phrases and images that come to mind when they hear the word 'sales' or 'sales rep'. Below are some examples of what they say:

- Smooth (but not in a good way)
- Don't listen
- Underhand
- Pushy
- Shiny suits
- Secondhand cars
- Dodgy
- Making you buy something that you don't want.

Not good is it? And it's unsurprising, therefore, that people feel uncomfortable about promoting their goods or services. With those kinds of feelings associated with sales, who would feel comfortable about selling anything?

The factor that really annoys people, however – the one that always comes top and with which everyone else in the room agrees – is the sales person's inability or reluctance to listen to what the customer wants.

Once I have allowed delegates to vent their spleen and disgorge themselves of all this pent-up anger and frustration, I go on to ask if they can recall a time when they were sold to and it was a good experience.

Thankfully, most can do this and once again, I hear the same positive characteristics repeated. The good sales people:

- Listened
- Were polite
- Were genuinely interested in what I wanted
- Knew their stuff
- Were able to give advice
- Suggested things that I'd not initially thought of
- Were helpful
- Took time with me

We have all experienced these kinds of sales people and quite likely left their company with less cash but very comfortable with the whole experience and our purchase. They exemplify something I said earlier – they made it easy for you to buy.

'People buy from people.' You may be familiar with that phrase and it's true. To be more accurate, one should add 'they like' or perhaps, 'they warm to'.

Why People Buy

You really do need to know why people are buying your product or service. Not just what they want, but what they need.

To explain the difference between wants and needs, I reckon the hackneyed old 'drill' story is worth trotting out. No one wants to own a drill and that includes people walking into B&Q right now and about to ask the guy in the orange apron: 'Excuse me, could you tell me where the drills are because I want to buy one?' Yes, they may *want* one, but the reason is that they *need* holes. And they need holes because they need to put Rawlplugs and screws in those holes in order to fix something to a wall. See the difference?

I have a drill; I bet you have a drill. And I bet you, like me, never, ever use it until you have need of a hole.

I don't pretend to be some kind of psychologist, but once you've spent enough time selling, sitting in front of potential customers, whether that be in a shop or out on the road and in their offices, you do begin to get a good feel for why a particular individual is buying something.

The most important thing to realize right from the start is that we purchase very little based solely on logical, practical reasons. We just can't help ourselves: we're creatures filled with emotion and we react emotionally to most purchases.

Not sure? Think about the stuff you have at home. In fact, think about your home. Did you buy that based on logical reasoning?

Or your car. No one buys a car based on logic. Blokes buy a car because of how a particular model makes them feel and based on how men and women will perceive them when they drive it or it's outside their house. Women are no different, but at least they tend to be more honest about their reasons. I asked a woman the other week why she'd opted for a particular motor and she said: 'Because it's got a nice friendly face.' Men will trot out a load of facts, statistics and terribly sensible reasons for choosing a certain model when all along it's because they want to demonstrate to other men how much money they're earning or how successful or outdoors and rugged they are. It's impossible to *not* communicate by the choices you make.

I do a lot of work with people in professional partnerships and, if I ask groups of lawyers or accountants why clients use their services, I normally get the same answer: 'They are buying our technical expertise and knowledge.' This is true, but it's not the whole answer. Why should I, as a client, be bothered about how clever you are as a lawyer or an accountant? The answer's simple: because then I don't need to worry about my accounts or legal issues – you'll handle all that. That's what clients are really paying for: comfort, security and peace of mind.

Think about your GP or family doctor for a moment. Mine's excellent. He listens to what I say, he seems to ask me relevant questions and he has a nice, reassuring, friendly manner that makes me feel like I'm an equal rather than beneath him. He never seems to rush the consultation either.

But ask me to rank him in terms of his knowledge of medicine and his clinical expertise compared to his fellow professionals and I haven't a clue whether he'd be top 10, top 50 or bottom 10 out of 100. And do you know what: it doesn't matter, as long as I feel better once I've been to see him and taken the course of treatment he's prescribed.

And so it is with those of you in professional services. It's not your knowledge your clients are after, it's the peace of mind and security that knowledge brings with it.

Similarly, emotion influences our choices about a whole host of products. We buy things because we believe they will:

- confer status
- boost our ego
- give us confidence
- make us like our peers
- make us more manly/feminine
- make us a better parent
- make us appear/feel youthful
- make us appear mature/older

Next time you're watching the television, notice how many ads are using one or several of these eight factors to persuade you to buy their product. Very few adverts attempt to influence our purchasing decisions by giving us logical reasons – they go straight for our emotions.

Justify What We Buy

So we buy with our heart or our gut, but then we justify the decision to ourselves logically.

Most people who live with a partner know that the secret is to get 'approval' to buy the item in question prior to purchase. This can sometimes take days, weeks or even months: a sort of persuasion by attrition. You do this so that come the day you walk in the house with your Manolo Blahnik shoes or 52-inch plasma television, it's not going to result in a full-blown row.

Equally, decisions are so much easier if we know others have made similar ones. We look for confirmation that what we are about to do is the right thing. Ever been asked to sponsor someone for charity? What's the first thing you look at when they hand you the form? That's right, how much others have given. Why? You're a free-thinking individual: you can give as much or as little as you want. But you don't. You give the 'going rate'. This is called 'social proof' and it's very powerful in persuading and influencing others.

How many times have you been out for a meal and been asked: 'What are you having?' or 'Are you having a starter?' Why do people want to know this? They're adults, they're going to pay for their own meal, they can have what they want – and yet they still ask. And they do so because they seek the assurance that what they are doing is not going to make them stand out from the norm.

The people you are selling to are no different: they too seek assurance. You can address that issue by mentioning that other clients, similar to them, are already using your service.

7

None of us makes decisions in isolation. We have to justify them to at least two people: ourselves and another person close to us. This other person may be our boss, a close friend or colleague, or our partner or parent.

When you are in a meeting with a prospect, it might be that she loves what you have to offer and imagines that working with you would be worthwhile, but she'll have to justify the decision to use you to someone else within the organization.

The fleet manager is in charge of purchasing the company vehicles, but she has to justify her choice to the finance director and maybe the managing director, and the drivers of the vehicles of course.

The human resources manager has to decide which recruitment agency to have on his preferred supplier list. This will be based on whether he trusts and gets on well with the person dealing with his account (assuming that this person can provide the candidates he seeks), but his boss will want to know that he has chosen wisely.

No one got sacked for choosing BMW or for buying a Canon copier or a Nokia phone or for sourcing lunch from Pret a Manger or Marks & Spencer.

Say I go to see the training and development manager at a large law firm and she likes what I do, feels that the courses are the right fit for her people, and we get on like a house on fire. In her mind she may think 'Yep, I'd like to use Nick', but she has to feel confident about putting me in front of a group of lawyers for a half or full day. If I'm no good it's not me that'll get it in the neck, it's her.

Knowing that's how it works means that when I meet a training and development manager for the first time, I make sure that I tell her things that give her confidence that I'm a pretty safe bet in front of lawyers. So I mention my experience working in law, the hundreds of lawyers I've helped secure new jobs for when in recruitment, and then

I name some of the law firms I now do training for. This builds my credibility and helps them to trust me. Although they still have to make a leap of faith when first using my services, it's only a small one. And provided I do a good job and the feedback reflects that, then they're happy to use me again.

Eventually, the relationship of trust is so strong that your customers will begin to ask for your advice about training issues and get you in to do stuff in front of potentially tricky audiences. And while all this is developing within the relationship, they are chatting to people who do the same job in other firms and recommending you, and from such conversations spring referrals – which is what every sales person wants, because it means they don't have to do as much networking or cold calling.

The Characteristics, Attributes and Qualities of Good Sales People

You're not a sales person – that's why you're reading this book. But you do have to sell and you want to get good at it. In fact, you want to be great at it. That's how you're going to grow your small business, or bring in revenue as a fee earner in your firm.

Some common qualities are shared by all brilliant sales people. So before we get into the techniques, how about we start by looking at the traits you should be emulating? Without exception, great sales people demonstrate the following:

- persistence
- always developing business
- a positive attitude
- an aversion to hard work

- belief in what they sell
- a definite but flexible focus

Persistence

Persistence means following up every lead, contact and referral until it results in business, is put on hold for another time or is ditched indefinitely.

Persistence is about doing something to develop sales and business every day, no matter how small: whether that's an email, a phone call, a coffee with a prospect, attending a networking event or delivering a seminar.

Persistence is about reading books, listening to audio CDs, attending seminars or training sessions that improve your business development skills.

Always Developing Business
You must do at least one business development activity every day.

Never, ever, ever, ever stop developing business. I have seen too many sales people ease back when times are good.

I don't give a monkey's how busy you are, you must be able to look back at your day and know that you did at least one thing that would lead you to more sales. This can be a phone call, an email or a letter, as we saw under persistence. It doesn't matter how small it is: send a brochure, follow up on a lead, ask someone for a referral, speak to someone outside the loo on a Virgin train. I did that once and the guy I got chatting to happened to be involved in the training department of a huge multinational insurance company.

So, whatever you do, don't ever go to bed without being able to answer 'yes' to the question: 'Did I do something to bring in another customer today?'

A Positive Attitude

Guess what: optimists are better at developing business than pessimists.

When a pessimist hears 'No thanks, we are really happy with our current supplier', he or she regards it as:

- Permanent – 'If they won't buy what I have now then they won't ever buy it.'
- Pervasive – 'If they won't buy from me then no one will.'
- Personal – 'It's me! They didn't buy what I had because they didn't like me.'

In contrast, an optimist thinks: 'Oh well, my timing's obviously not right, I'll make a note to get in touch with them in six months' time. Right: on to my next prospect.'

In fact, an optimist goes one step further. Having conceded that the timing is obviously not right, he (or she) tells the prospect that he'll leave them with the information he's been discussing and makes a note in his diary – so the prospect can see him do it – that he'll drop them a line in three or six months' time.

An Aversion to Hard Work

Every sales person I have ever met is lazy at heart (why do you think they're in sales?). As long as you hit your targets, your time is pretty much your own when you're a sales rep. Lunch when you fancy it, start and end the day when you want, and play loads of golf and declare it as 'client entertainment' or 'business development' or 'account management' on your time sheet!

But that does not mean they shy away from hard work or are in some way not 100% dedicated to the cause. Far from it!

Sales people are interested in selling as much stuff with the minimum amount of effort and in the shortest possible time, which means that they don't work hard: they work *smart*.

A Belief in What They Sell

If you are currently working for an organization and are attempting to persuade people to buy what you do or have and don't believe in either the product or organization, then leave now. I'm serious. You're wasting everyone's time.

There have been three times I have attempted to sell things I didn't believe in and things didn't turn out well on any occasion.

A Definite But Flexible Focus

Good developers of business have a target. I don't just mean a figure, I mean a market. They know, before they set out in the morning, before they send the first email, write the first letter, or make the first telephone call, which organizations in which sectors they are going to contact.

They *do not* think they can sell everything they have to offer to just anyone; they have a target to aim for.

However, because their income depends on being successful, they retain the flexibility to change target if it becomes clear that they can hit their monetary goal more quickly.

Having a target is the single most important aspect of developing business, which is why I dedicate an entire chapter to it.

Perhaps this is a good point to let you know that reading this book isn't going to make you even half decent at winning work. In order to do that, you're going to have to get up off your backside and do stuff, so let's start here – but because it's early days, you can stay seated.

THE STUFF YOU HATE . . . SELLING

Grab a pen, pencil or other equally convenient writing instrument and jot down the traits and characteristics you already posses that you reckon will be handy when developing business.

Once that's sorted, write down those that you are going to have to address because they aren't terribly conducive to being a business development whizzkid.

Now you can read the next chapter.

CHAPTER 2

INTRODUCING THE TARGET, CONNECT, MEET, ASK MODEL

I've witnessed and heard of many delaying tactics employed by people keen to put off the day when they actually start selling. I can't blame them and won't blame you if you've been doing the same, because we all put off doing the things we hate.

However, getting started is a whole lot easier if you know what to do first.

Do you drive? Remember the process by which you were taught, the step-by-step process of 'Mirror, Signal, Manoeuvre'?

Well, here's a process for developing business: *TARGET, CONNECT, MEET, ASK* (and *FOLLOW UP* at every stage). I'm going to introduce you to the model in this chapter so that once you've read it, you'll be able to get going and start building your business right away.

Early in 2010, one of my clients asked me to come up with a model for the business development process I use when, well, er . . . developing business. My initial response was that I didn't have one; that what I did was just instinctive, after years of refining how I go about selling. However, he pressed me on the subject and said that if I could define what I did in terms of a process, it would be something he and I could roll out to partners.

So I got thinking. I really thought about what it is that I do. And it was tricky.

However, I realized that I do follow a process, pretty much to the letter and pretty much all of the time:

1. *TARGET*   }
2. *CONNECT*   }   *FOLLOW UP*
3. *MEET*   }
4. *ASK*   }

I *TARGET* the sectors I want to sell to and then the decision makers, I then *CONNECT* with the sole purpose of arranging to *MEET* them, where, after listening to them, I *ASK* for their business. And at every single stage of the process I *FOLLOW UP*.

I'm going to go into loads of detail about every stage in the rest of this book, so that by the end of each chapter you'll know what to be doing next. But I reckon a quick look at the whole model (or a 'heads up', for those of you who love banal business jargon) might be in order now.

Target

You absolutely have to have a focus for your business development activity. You can't wander blindly into the market thinking: 'Ooh, this is lovely; I could sell my stuff to loads of people who'll all love it' or 'Everyone needs what I have so my market is massive'. While this might give you a warm, fuzzy glow about how much money you're going to make, you'll just end up throwing a lot of business development hard work at a wall in the hope that enough of it will stick – and trust me, not enough of it will.

Having a target to aim for is imperative and is the very first thing you must consider.

Which markets are you going to go for, which organizations, and which people within those organizations?

Connect

What I'm talking about here is connecting emotionally with the people you want to persuade to buy your product or service.

Making an emotional connection with prospective purchasers is terribly important and yet so few people even make an attempt to do it.

If you begin regarding selling as a science and stop doing it instinctively, you focus on coming across as professional. And while being professional is important because it builds trust and conveys credibility to your potential customer, the fact is that in endeavouring to appear professional, you almost always simply give the impression of being very earnest and a bit 'up yourself'.

Think about all the emails, letters, flyers and phone calls you have received either at home or at work, sent by organizations or individuals trying to sell you their wares. What happens to them? You delete them, bin or recycle them, or hang up. And you do that because they have failed to make any sort of emotional connection with you.

I want you to appreciate that *CONNECT* refers to any kind of contact with a potential client.

There are numerous ways to connect with the people you want to persuade. Along with the ones already mentioned, email, phone and letter, I'd add video conferencing, Skype, LinkedIn, Facebook, speaking at a conference or seminar, or meeting people face to face at a networking event.

Meet

The third part of the process is *MEET*, which anyone serious about selling is aiming for when they initially connect with their target.

Irrespective of how you go about connecting, it's with one specific purpose in mind: to meet the person who can sign the order, give the green light, say 'yes', give the thumbs up, release the funds, let slip the dogs of war . . . sorry, I got all Shakespearean for a moment there.

Emailing people won't do. Sending flyers out is hit and miss. Producing a glossy newsletter/bulletin/pamphlet/email is akin to staking your financial security on a Euro Millions ticket.

You absolutely, completely, utterly and most assuredly have to meet the person you want to win work from, especially if you are selling a service, because you are the product.

Those of you quick off the mark will realize that one way to connect *and* meet at the same time is at a networking event; and you'd be right. However, in all but the most exceptional cases – it's never happened to me – an encounter at a networking event is not going to be as productive as a one-to-one, pre-arranged chat over a coffee, which both parties have agreed and are aware is going to be about learning whether a supplier–purchaser relationship might be on the cards.

Ask

If you don't ask for the order – and the vast majority of people don't – how are you going to get the answer 'yes'?

There are ways to ask that aren't as abrupt as the business equivalent of blurting out: 'So, do you fancy a snog?' And there are ways to handle the objections that such an approach is almost inevitably going to lead to, which even more subtle approaches may prompt.

People are reluctant to ask because they fear rejection and that dreaded response: 'Thanks but no thanks.' However, that's not the end of the world and anyway, 'No' in this context doesn't mean 'No', it just means 'Not at the moment'.

Very often, when you ask for the business, the job, the order or the contract, the question of price arises – 'How much does it cost?' Once again, this is an issue about which many people worry, even though a query about price is actually a positive thing.

Other issues or objections may arise. An objection is merely a blockage to agreeing on a deal. While the emergence of objections can seem to be a catastrophe to anyone new to developing business, it's better to have them out in the open and thus able to be dealt with, than not to know the reason for not securing the order.

Following Up

Following up is something you need to be doing right through the business development process. It's the umbrella under which you do *TARGETING, CONNECTING, MEETING* and *ASKING*.

If your job or income relies on persuading others to buy what you have, then you must follow up on anything and everything that comes your way that will help you make inroads into your target market.

Leads will also appear that take you into different markets and that's fine, so long as they are profitable and don't mean you having to make major adaptations to your product or service.

So follow up, all the time, every time and with a determined focus. **Do not leave loose ends**!

You'll know you're following up well when your diary is peppered with reminders to call, email and write to people you've previously made contact with.

FOLLOW UP also happens to be the part of the business development process with which a hell of a lot of people struggle. They really hate it, a lot.

There are a number of reasons for this, but the biggest is that they worry about coming across as too pushy, so they tend not to bother at all.

Well, don't worry, because later on I'm going to devote an awful lot of space to explaining in detail how to follow up efficiently, effectively and elegantly, while keeping in control and focused throughout.

And because following up is something you should be doing after every stage of the model, I'll have a paragraph or two at the end of each chapter as well.

OK, before you can even think about following up, you first need to know who you want to be following up with – and that means deciding who to target.

CHAPTER 3

TARGET (WHO, WHICH, WHAT)

WHO YOU WANT TO SELL TO, IN WHICH ORGANIZATIONS, IN WHAT SECTORS

D o you hate the whole selling thing because you seem to be pursuing numerous potential sales-generating avenues and have got yourself into a bit of a mess: whenever you set aside time to developing business, you have no idea which avenue to go down?

In this chapter we're going to take a look at *TARGETING*: the focus or goal that's going to get you out of bed each day committing yourself to *CONNECTING* with some people (the *right* people, of course).

By the end of the chapter, you'll know why it's essential to have a target, how to get one, which people should be targeted and why.

You must appreciate that no self-respecting sales person would dream of making a single phone call, sending one email, attending a networking event or even getting out of bed on a Monday morning, if they didn't know exactly who they were going to target.

Getting Started: A Definite But Flexible Focus

Why Definite?

You must have a defined target market.

When you're first setting out to win business, it's tempting and somehow more reassuring if you tell yourself that there are loads and loads of people to whom you could be selling. This, however, is a false sense of security and will have you doing lots of activity but with little reward. In other words, if you try to target everyone, you'll spread your activity too thin and achieve nothing.

It's a bit like packing your suitcase and showing up at the airport. You want to go away, because you need to unwind. You could, in theory, go anywhere to achieve that. So there you are, staring at the departures board thinking: 'Great, look at all the places I can go!'

But you can only go one place at a time and if you haven't decided where, then you won't know which departure gate to go to. That means you'll wander around the airport, wasting lots of time and energy but not actually getting very far. However, if you know your ultimate destination, then you know where to target your effort.

It's no different when developing business. You need to make lots of effort to hit the target you've chosen, but you can only hit one or maybe two at the same time with any real impact.

Why Flexible?

While you should set out with your eye on a specific target, you also need to be flexible enough to adapt if you're not getting the results you want or had anticipated.

At the end of the day, you sell to make money. If you aren't making money from your target market, you need to pick another one. And sometimes, although you set off in one direction, opportunities in an area you had never considered arise; in which case, grab them!

I've been self-employed four times in my life. That means I have woken up on a Monday morning with absolutely no income other than that which I can generate. This must be the urban equivalent of being dropped in a jungle with nothing but what you learnt at Survival School. It's frightening and yet incredibly exciting and it makes you feel alive. Those of you who have recently started your business will know precisely what I mean.

In this situation you are faced with two choices: go bust once the money runs out or get very good at developing business, very quickly!

Even if you're employed, there is still pressure to bring in more work. Indeed, in order to advance in many of the professions – law, accountancy and engineering, for example – you have to 'show them the money' if you are to stand a chance of partnership.

So, whether you're sitting at a desk in an office or at your kitchen table, where do you start?

Your Target List

You need to make a target list. I mean an actual, written-down list. The mere act of writing something down seeks to enforce that which you have committed to paper. Anyone can promise to do something, but just to be sure they do, we often ask them to 'put it in writing' because we know it's more of a commitment.

I want you to think of all the people who would possibly be interested in buying the product or service you provide. Furthermore, think about whether they'd either be 'well up for it' and therefore *HOT*, or 'really not bothered' and thus *COLD*. As you work through this chapter, begin to consider how likely they are to buy from you.

Perhaps the analogy of hot plates on top of a cooker might be helpful at this juncture? (It's a rhetorical question, so I've given you a diagram of one!)

Before I give you a thorough explanation of what I mean by each one, here's a quick overview:

- *HOT* – people who already pay for what you do.
- *WARM* – people you know or people who buy from your organization but not what you provide.
- *TEPID* – Referrals and organizations that supply you.
- *COLD* – Businesses or organizations with which you have no connection.

Credibility and Trust

You target in this order: *HOT, WARM, TEPID, COLD.* There are two reasons for this – trust and credibility – and if you don't have either of these you're stuffed.

Selling is essentially about persuading someone or having influence over them. In order to stand any chance of doing either, the person you seek to influence must regard you as credible and, above all, they must trust you.

Think about the relationship you have with your friends. They can easily persuade you to change your mind and go out for a Chinese rather than an Indian. Or they may have influence over you to the extent that you might be persuaded to take a particular holiday or buy a particular car or even go out with someone. If there was an absence of trust between you, then they wouldn't stand a chance, would they?

In business, it is your experience and skill that give you credibility. It is your qualifications and your client list. That's why companies display 'By Royal Appointment' crests.

Trust, however, is earned over time and beats credibility hands down. You can be the world's leading expert in something, but if people don't trust you, you stand no chance of persuading them to buy from you.

27

It is the absence of these two elements that makes cold calling so tricky. That's why great sales people excel at establishing both really quickly and always look for referrals.

With that understood, let's look at the four kinds of target.

HOT: Your Existing Customers

This market is made up of people and organizations that already buy your services or products and with whom you have an existing relationship. They *trust* you, regard you as having *credibility* and are therefore more likely to buy more stuff from you: new products, a different service and so on.

WARM: Customers of the Organization in Which You Work

Say that I'm a lettings agent in an estate agency that offers many other services: property maintenance, the sale and purchase of property and mortgage advice. I already have a portfolio of loyal clients. Before attempting to win brand new clients (that is, those who have no dealings with any part of the firm), it makes sense to approach those who already use the agency's services but not yet the lettings department. Why? Because they already *trust* the firm and know it to be *credible*. It's your duty to let clients of the firm know about all the other stuff you can do for them. Sure, not everyone is going to want to let out their property, but you'll only know for sure if you approach them.

We are all wildly busy. We like it if we can get everything under 'one roof'; not always, I admit, but at least it's nice to be given the choice. This is why price comparison sites have done so well: they work on the principle that you can compare an awful lot of prices in one hit.

The bottom line is, don't waste your time going after new clients until you are sure your existing ones know about all you do and that it would be in their interest to buy it from you.

If you have just started running your own business, you only have a warm market, which is anyone who knows you: friends, family, ex-colleagues and contacts (assuming you aren't restricted from contacting them). And when you are asking all of these people for work, remember to ask them if they know anyone who would be interested in what you are offering.

Remember, *HOT* people are those who are already buying from you; in other words, handing over cash for what you offer. Friends and family are close, but don't assume they'll want what you are offering. And even if they buy from you once in order to help you get things going, they may not buy from you again.

Show Them That You Love Them

In addition to tackling your hot and warm markets because of the presence of oodles of trust and credibility, there's another factor at play and that's *love*. You love them and they want to know that you do; and what's more, they want to give some lovin' right back to you.

I use the word *love* on purpose.

A few years back the CEO of a large firm in the Midlands told me that his firm had lost a client. When he asked the managing director of that company why it was no longer using his firm's services, he replied: 'Because you don't love us any more.'

When the CEO asked him to illuminate, he said that when the firm was originally looking to win his business, his people had been told that they were special, beautiful and lovely, and that the firm would treasure their business and work hard to keep things just so. But as the years had gone on, the firm had gradually stopped paying them as much attention, to a point where they now felt that their business was being taken for granted. All the while the magic and sparkle were fading, another, rival firm had been gently wooing and courting the CEO's client. This new firm had told people that they were beautiful, special and lovely and that they would be showered with attention and love. So guess what? Yep, they went with the competitor.

Don't ever take your clients for granted. They need to know that you still want them. Sending emailed articles doesn't count, though! How loved would you feel if your partner kept in touch via a newsletter?

Many, many organizations boast that they 'go the extra mile'. Many people within such organizations say that they 'go out of their way' to help clients, that they are there at the convenience of the client. They seldom actually deliver, however.

Sometimes, 'going the extra mile' means literally that. Your competitors can't be bothered – make sure that you are and you'll shine!

And remember this: every single day of the week your customers and clients are being chatted up by your competitors. Imagine if that was happening to your partner: you'd definitely make sure they knew how much you loved them and not take them for granted. We all like being told we are desirable and still wanted – punters are no different.

They Want to Give You More Work (Because They Love You Right Back)

Your existing clients expect you to ask them for more work and they want to give it to you.

Some time ago I was sharing a coffee with the marketing director of a large and very reputable professional services company that had recently spent a small fortune on a client survey, in order to find out what customers thought about the level of service, the price they were paying, the competency of the fee earners and so on. All was glowing: the clients loved the company. Only one area of concern had emerged.

A number of clients had said that they wondered why the firm had not asked for more work from them!

That's a '*What*?!' moment, isn't it?

TEPID: Referrals

I like the word 'tepid'. It's fallen out of fashion of late, being replaced by the ever-present 'lukewarm'. Tepid harks back to a more innocent age, when things were measured in 'tbs' and 'oz' and 'tsps', when mums would dip their elbow to test the temperature of the water in the bath to make sure it was OK for their infant.

Your tepid market is made up of organizations or people who come to your attention by way of a referral. However, some referrals are warmer than others; 'more tepid' or 'tepider', if you will.

I would suggest that someone who is referred to you – through a recommendation such as 'Hey Dave, you should get in touch with Sally because she's a great life-coach' – is a warmer and thus more positive referral than the other way around: 'Sally, you should give Dave a ring because he was only saying the other day that he felt he was in a bit of a rut work-wise and could do with some advice on what to do with his life.'

In the former, if Dave does contact Sally he has made a positive step and is halfway to doing business with her; whereas in the latter, it's Sally who's going to have to do the chasing.

Referrals are something you should be going after all the time, especially in the early days of developing business. Once you've established yourself your name will spread within your target market(s) and you'll notice just how much referral work comes your way.

My own experience (and I can't say if this is the same in other sectors/industries) has been that it was following three years of pretty much constant business development activity that I noticed a steady stream of referral work, which meant that I could ease down on the proactive stuff.

I'm sure all businesses arrive at some sort of critical mass or 'tipping point' at which there is sufficient referral business to keep you busy, although I'd never become complacent, because things are wont to change very rapidly in business. And anyway, stopping any business development activity just doesn't sit well with me and neither should it with you!

How Do You Get Referrals?

I use two ways to get referrals:

- I have a firm on my target list and ask my existing clients if they know the person responsible for training and development and, if they do, whether they would help me by affording me an introduction – normally via email.
- I ask my very good clients if they can think of any firms that I should be approaching and if they could facilitate an introduction.

It goes without saying that you must have a very good relationship in order for the first way to be successful, but even more so in the case of the second.

Sales people are always looking and asking for referrals. I reciprocate clients' efforts on my behalf by giving them a big discount off my normal daily rate and by doing occasional 30- to 45-minute one-to-one coaching session for senior people within their organizations for free. Once you build good relationships with people, asking for referrals or for help breaking into new clients becomes a whole lot easier.

Referrals are something that will bring results once you have established a solid working and, often, friendship-type relationship with your client, so in the early days of your business development activity you might have to rely on a great deal more cold calling.

Warning: Clients will only feel comfortable referring their contacts or friends to you once they really trust you, because if you mess up you could cause great embarrassment to them for having recommended you. Be sure to go that extra, extra mile for those recommended by others.

And don't forget those organizations from which you purchase goods or services. I'm not talking about your energy provider or the insurance company, but rather an organization where you have a personal relationship with an individual. So not the Ford Motor Company, but the guy who you bought your car from or the dealership manager. If you're a baker, not the firm from which you buy the flour but the rep with whom you deal. See what I mean?

These connections may not be hot, but there is nevertheless a connection. You buy their services or products, so why shouldn't they buy yours? Hey, it's always worth asking.

COLD – People With Whom You Have No Connection

This market is made up of people with whom you have no connection: you and your organization haven't done business with them and you haven't been referred to them or vice versa.

However, as with the tepid bit of your potential market, it is possible to divide 'cold' into 'slightly chilly and 'bleedin' freezing'.

'Slightly Chilly'

Say you manufacture funky desk and table lamps and when you began your business you opted to target hotels. You now do loads of work with hotels, and have bags of experience and a detailed understanding of how they work and function.

The vast majority of large hotels are in London, so at first you concentrated your efforts within that geographical area, but now you wish to expand your business development activity and you figure that sticking with hotels in other cities makes sense.

Some of you might be thinking that if you have no connection with them, even if they are in the same sector, surely that puts them in the 'bleedin' freezing' category. But I say 'no'.

If you are working in a relatively small market, in a relatively small geographical area, then the chances are that your existing clients or customers will know people within the same sector, which is probably the case within the hotel trade. The community of hotel procurement managers must be relatively small – after all, how many hotels are large enough to justify employing a person dedicated to procurement? Fifty? A hundred? Given that you could sell lamps to every household and organization in the UK, these are piddlingly little numbers.

So when contacting a hotel outside of London, you want to mention the names of other hotels you already supply as well as the names of individual purchasing managers, working on the principle that there's a fair chance the person you're talking to will know them. And by name dropping, you establish trust and credibility with an audience to whom the names mean something.

Ask yourselves these questions:

1. In which markets or sectors do I work at the moment?
2. Do I make money in those markets?
3. Do I like working in those markets?
4. Do I work with everyone within those sectors?

If the answer to number 2 and 3 is 'yes' but it's a big fat 'no' to number 4, then that's where you want to be targeting.

'Bleedin' Freezing

This is what I'd call cold calling in the true sense of the phrase. This market is massive, but it's the hardest one to get results from, because it consists of organizations in sectors to which you have no connection other than that you've seen their name on the web, in a directory, mentioned in the press or on the side of a van.

You lack credibility – at least within their sector – and that makes it harder for them to trust you. Of course – sticking with the lamps for hotels scenario – dropping names such as Hilton, Holiday Inn and Radisson will help, since most people have heard of them.

Following Up

Such is the importance of having a defined target that I am going ask you to think about any competitive game. Virtually every sport you can think of has a goal – some literally.

How would Usain Bolt get on if he just knew he wanted to run fast? Without a defined distance and a finishing line at the end, he'd look a bit daft. As what would the Rooneys, Ronaldos and all those other talented football players do if they ran onto a pitch without any goal posts? Sure, they can demonstrate loads of skills, fantastic ball control, mind-blowing headers – but those are all a waste of time if the players don't know what they are aiming for.

Your business activity has to be aimed at something, otherwise you're either plagued with inertia because you don't know which should be your first step, or you're running round like an idiot hoping that your haphazard, scatter-gun approach might eventually hit something.

Now, although the targeting bit of the model is the one where you haven't connected with anyone yet, do be sure to *FOLLOW UP* with those people in your markets – most likely your warm and tepid sectors – who have said they will connect/introduce you to their contacts.

If you approach someone and ask them to refer you to a friend or ask a colleague if she'll set up a meeting for the pair of you to meet with one of her clients and she agrees, go one step further and ask her according to what timescale she intends doing so. The conversation goes something like this:

> **YOU:** *Hi Sara, I'm targeting people within the beauty sector and wondered if you could help me by introducing me to any of your clients you think might be interested in what I do.*
>
> **SARA:** *Sure, L'Oréal and P&G might be worth meeting and I have great relationships with a number of the senior people at both. I'll drop them an email and let them know you'll be in touch.*
>
> **YOU:** *Cheers. I'm keen not to get in touch with them before you've let them know - no one likes the cold approach - so just to make sure my timing's right, how long should I leave it: two to three days or a week or so?*
>
> **SARA:** *Oh, I'll drop them an email before the end of this week.*
>
> **YOU:** *Great. In that case I'll probably contact them the middle of next week. Thanks very much.*

By getting Sara to commit to a time, even though it's not specific, it puts her under a little more pressure to deliver on her promise because she committed to help you. This works because we all strive to be consistent; if she doesn't do what she said she would, she will be being inconsistent.

Get into the habit of asking for people's help at every stage of the business development process. Help is a compelling word, in that it's very difficult for someone to say 'no' to.

If you haven't done so already, write down a list of people and/or organizations in your market. Once you've done that, mark them *HOT, WARM, TEPID* or *COLD* and note down which names on the *HOT* and *WARM* lists might be able to help you with referrals.

Once you have this list and thus a focus for your activity, you'll find that work begins to come from all kinds of markets you never anticipated.

The following quote sums it all up nicely. The main text is often attributed to Goethe. However, the U.S. Goethe society claims that it is in fact by a guy called W.H. Murray, writing in *The Scottish Himalayan Expedition,* 1951,

But when I said that nothing had been done I erred in one important matter. We had definitely committed our- selves and were halfway out of our ruts. We had put down our passage money - booked a sailing to Bombay. This may sound too simple, but is great in consequence. Until one is committed, there is hesitancy, the chance to draw back, always ineffectiveness. Concerning all acts of initiative (and creation), there is one elementary truth the ignorance of which kills countless ideas and splendid plans: that the moment one definitely commits oneself, then providence moves too. A whole stream of events issues from the decision, raising in one's favour all manner of unforeseen incidents, meetings and mate- rial assistance, which no man could have dreamt would have come his way. I learned a deep respect for one of Goethe's couplets:
Whatever you can do or dream you can, begin it.
Boldness has genius, power and magic in it!

And that's exactly what will happen to you once you have a definite focus: 'a whole stream of events issues from the decision'.

It's also a whole lot easier and more effective to establish a great reputation within one, specialist field than to try and be all things to all sectors, because even when you do concentrate all your energies in one sector, be that geographical, professional or industrial, you will inevitably be asked to do work in others.

Once you have your list of targets you move to the second part of the model, *CONNECT*.

CHAPTER 4

CONNECT

MAKING AN EMOTIONAL
CONNECTION TO SECURE
THAT MEETING

A nother aspect of developing business that many people hate is getting in touch with the people they really should meet, connecting with them. They hate it because they worry about being too pushy, but also because they approach the entire exercise with a mentality that says: 'Why would anybody want to buy what I've got, there are so many other people doing miles better stuff than I/we do and anyway ours isn't the best.' All too often they just send out either a paper or email 'flyer', in the vain hope that if they send enough someone is bound to reply. Or they imagine that if they attend enough networking events (more of this later) the same effect will occur. Well, it won't.

Let me make something really clear. This book is about sales and developing business *face to face*. There are other books that deal with online and mail-order businesses. This isn't one of them, principally because I have no experience of either.

Selling face to face means that once you've decided on your target – the person you need to meet – every action you take is with one purpose in mind: securing a meeting with that person.

That is why this chapter is about how you go about doing that in the most effective way. How do you connect with the person in order to maximize your chances of getting between 30 and 60 minutes of one-to-one time with them, chatting over a tea or coffee?

I don't mean meeting them at a networking event, which is why I regard networking as simply one of the ways to 'connect' with people. Sure, there will be occasions when you hook up with someone at an event and the encounter goes beyond small talk and into business and how you might be able to help them. However, I would suggest that even on those rare occasions, you'll still need to arrange to meet them again in a calmer environment (in other words, 'follow up') where you won't be interrupted by others and there isn't the pressure to move on and get chatting to other attendees.

I deal with that sort of meeting in the next chapter, cunningly – and rather cleverly I feel – called '*MEET*'.

Back to *CONNECT*. If you want to make it easy for people to set aside time to meet you and, hopefully, ultimately buy from you, you're going to have to contact them in a manner that makes an emotional connection. Making such a connection is the absolute key to successful business development and yet it is something far too many people fail to do.

There are several methods you can use, but by far the most popular are:

- Phone
- Letter
- Email
- Network (social: LinkedIn etc.)
- Network (at an event)
- Present/speak (formally)

It's my intention to talk about each one here except networking, to which I have devoted a separate chapter. It's a training course all on its own and it's a big subject about which people have umpteen questions.

Let's kick off with the trickiest but perhaps most effective and definitely the quickest way to connect with people – the phone call.

The Cold Call

Cold calling is *the* most feared type of call.

Talking about cold calling may seem a bit odd, since you've just read a chapter that advises you to avoid it like the plague. However, I'm covering this topic here for four reasons.

First, you are not allowed to use a calculator at school until you have been taught and have mastered mental arithmetic, because it forms the basis of so much of what you do as an adult in navigating your way through life. So it is with selling. Understanding the process and thinking behind cold calling ensures that you have a better understanding of all other parts of connecting with people; it's the foundation on which so much of business development is built.

Secondly, unless you are dead lucky, you are bound to have to do some cold calling when you start developing business. And if you are ever unlucky enough to have the backside fall out of your business (the equivalent of your calculator going AWOL), you'll have no option but to pick up the phone and call people you don't know.

My dad ran a marketing business in the 1980s. It was doing well, but then the business dried up and the bank wanted to shut him down. He sat on the bed, opened the Yellow Pages and made phone calls – cold. He landed his biggest *ever* client by doing that, a client that saw his business thrive. He made a small fortune. When the crap hits the fan and the fan is switched on (real messy), the ability to make cold calls can make it all smell nice again, so you need to know how to do it, properly.

Thirdly, whenever I'm asked to teach people how to develop business, whether that's one-to-one coaching, with a room full of delegates in a regular training session or to hundreds of people attending a conference, people always want to know how to cold call well.

And finally, I've devoted a lot of page space to all aspects of telephoning because there are so many variables involved in connecting directly with another person. Even if the person you want to get to meet is not in, you'll always end up speaking to a receptionist or, if you get further, a PA, secretary or work colleague.

So, I am going to take you through a step-by-step process of how to cold call, as well as explaining why you should do it the way I'm suggesting.

Getting the Name of the Right Person to Meet – The M.A.N.

I was first introduced to this 'person' when I was taught selling back in 1987. It was drummed into us by a great guy called John Mifflin, who said that we should always be looking to get in front of the person with the Money, Authority and Need. In other words, we should get to meet the person in the position that possesses all three.

While referring to this individual as the M.A.N. is probably politically incorrect and in contravention of heaven knows how many EU directives, the point is made.

Step One: Have Your Target List in Front of You

You don't need your whole target list, what I'm talking about here is roughly ten names. Don't fret if circumstances dictate that you can only call two or three, it's just that if you have a decent number you'll be able to establish a kind of momentum or rhythm, which makes it so much easier – the first call is always and will always be the hardest.

Have a pen or pencil and some paper handy because you'll want to write stuff down. Then . . .

Ask yourself what you want from the call. That's easy. There is only one reason you are making this call: in order to arrange to *MEET* the other person. But you are going to do that in two separate calls. So your ultimate aim is to *MEET* them, but your first goal is simply to find out who it is you need to meet.

Step Two: Go Somewhere Private

Making a telephone call to someone you don't know is not a spectator sport. It's something to be done in private, away from others, and while standing up and quite possibly pacing about the room.

Most sales people have worked in offices with rows of desks populated by their colleagues, and taken part in the 'who can get the most appointments' competition. I can tell you, that's not for everyone and can make you feel awkward, embarrassed and exceptionally self-conscious, so please, do your cold calling away from others. That way, if you mess it up – and chances are you will the first couple of calls you make – it'll be your secret.

In addition, standing up will make you feel more confident and speak more clearly.

Step Three: Get Their Name and Title

You might be worried that the first call is really hard, but worry not: it's dead easy.

All you want to get from the first call is the name and title of the person who is responsible for buying what it is you're selling.

In my case, when I started my business I wanted to find out who was responsible for training and development, along with a few simple but really important details:

- Their full job title – 'Head of Learning and Development' or was it 'Director of Training and Learning'?

- Their title – Ms, Miss, Mrs, Mr, Dr etc.
- Their full name – *always ask how you spell their name.*

In practice the call sounds like this:

> **YOU:** *Good morning. I wonder if you could help me. I'm trying to find out the name of the person who is responsible for training and development within the firm. I don't need to speak to them, I just need their name.*
>
> **THEM:** *Yes, can I ask what it's regarding?*
>
> **YOU:** *Sure, I need to send them something in the post.*

It has to be said that it's rare anyone will ask me what it's regarding. Most of the time they'll give me the name of the person and then it's just left for me to check the details I've listed above.

It really doesn't matter what business you are in, the sequence and patter are pretty much the same:

> **YOU:** *I wonder if you can help* me; I'm trying to find out the name of the catering manager/procurement manager/fleet manager/head of marketing/facilities manager etc.*

*There's that word again!

You do not want to talk to the person at this point – even if the receptionist or secretary has asked you if you'd like to be put through. You are going to call them when you are good and ready and in the correct state of mind; being put through when you have not prepared is never a good idea.

One of the roles of receptionists and secretaries is to act as a kind of 'gatekeeper' to their colleagues within the office. Every organization receives countless calls a day from sales reps and if every one was put through, the fear is that no work would get done, so those at the front line, taking the calls, are there to filter out the rubbish.

If I call and ask for the name of the training and development manager, then it's pretty obvious that I don't know them and that I'm cold calling!

So wait a day – if you phone too soon after your initial 'fact-finding' call, there's a good chance they will recognize your voice and realize you are selling something.

By the way, if, when you call, the person you talk to offers more information than you were after, do take it! So if they ask if you'd like the training and development manager's direct dial number or email address, say 'Yes please' and thank them for their help.

If the organization has more than one office, then do check at which one your 'contact' is located.

Step Four: Call the Person You Want to Meet

There are times when it's better to call than others. All I'd say is this: think about the times of day when you really could do without a phone call and assume that other people are just the same, because they are.

So never call first thing in the morning, especially on a Monday. It takes us all an hour or so to settle in to the working day. We need a tea or a coffee, to open the mail, take a look at our inbox and maybe catch up on stuff with immediate colleagues.

I call people between about 10.30 and 11.30 am or 2.30 and 4.30 pm.

I must confess that I have to be in the mood to make the initial call to the person I want to see, but one thing's for sure, no matter how many times I've done it I always feel a bit nervous. So don't worry if you do too: it's normal.

What I will tell you, though, is that once you have made a call that results in you getting through to the person and securing a date to meet up, you'll be elated. It's then easy to whizz through the rest of the people on your list. That's one of the reasons I advise you to list the names of all the people you want to speak to, so that you can go through them really quickly and establish a rhythm and momentum.

Furthermore, once you have one meeting arranged, you can mention that on subsequent calls. Remember what I said earlier about social proof? If the person you are calling knows that their opposite number at a firm in the same sector in the same area is seeing you, they feel far more inclined to meet you too, not wanting to 'miss out'.

Increasing your chances of getting through to the right person

Let's say that the guy you want to meet is called Roger Moore. You make the call, it is answered by the receptionist and you ask to be put through to 'Roger'.

If there is more than one person with that name working there, the receptionist will ask: 'Which one?' To which you say: 'Roger, Roger Moore.'

The point is that when you ask for Roger, you should say it in a way that gives the impression you've known him for years; if you had, you'd probably just ask for 'Roger'.

I reckon I get put straight through to the person I want 50% of the time, simply by sounding authoritative and matter-of-fact – as though I speak to my 'contact' every day of the week.

The other 50% of the time you'll get asked: 'What is it regarding?' In that case you must reply honestly and say: 'I want to arrange to pop in and see him.'

It's vital that you are up front about your motives here and that you focus on what you want to achieve: namely, an appointment to see the person.

In many cases, the receptionist will put you through to the PA rather than the person you asked for.

Step Five: Talking to the PA

Personal assistants and secretaries are great people to strike up a relationship with because if they like you, they'll go out of their way to get you in front of their boss.

A few years ago I spent three months trying to secure a meeting with the head of learning and development of a leading national law firm, only to have every request ignored, whether via email, telephone or letter. Each time I called I ended up talking to his PA, who I got to know quite well over those 12 weeks. It got to a point where not only did she feel sorry for me, she thought her boss was being rude for not having acknowledged me, so she sent him an email (and copied me in!) in an amusing but quite forthright style, telling him that she thought he'd been impolite and that he should contact me immediately to set up a meeting – which he promptly did.

The thing to bear in mind is not to give them a load of bullshit or, far worse, take an authoritative and dismissive tone. Not only is it ignorant, but it's commercially stupid: PAs know more about their boss's diary than the boss does. And what is more, if the PA doesn't like you, you don't stand a chance of ever getting to see the boss.

If you get put through to a PA or secretary, this is the how the conversation normally goes:

> **PA:** *Hello, Roger Moore's office. How can I help you?*
>
> **You:** *Hi, is Roger in the office this morning?*
>
> **PA:** *Can I ask what it's regarding?*
>
> **You:** *Yes, I'm trying to fix up a time to meet up with him for a coffee.*
>
> **PA:** *Will he know what it's regarding?*

YOU: *No, he'll have no idea, we've never met before, which is why I want to pop in and see him. I'm a former lawyer, but I now spend my time teaching lawyers from the very junior to senior level in a range of communication skills. I wanted to find out how Roger goes about coordinating and organizing training within the firm and to see whether what I do might be of help. I'm seeing BLP on the 3rd and A&O on the 4th and wondered if he was free on either the 5th or 6th?*

It's been my experience that secretaries and PAs will appreciate your candour and therefore be quite helpful in suggesting how best to go about securing a meeting.

The PA may suggest that you send information:

PA: *Do you have a brochure?*

YOU: *Yes, would you like me to send him a copy?*

PA: *Yes, that would be useful and then I can pass it on to him.*

YOU: *Great. Shall I mark it for your attention or his?*

Or you may be put straight through.

Step Six: When You Get Through

You need to keep what you say short, sweet and to the point. Sure, it may turn out that there is opportunity for small talk, in which case be prepared to indulge in a little, but whatever you do, do not waste your prospect's time.

Getting to the point

Once you've done this a few times you will develop a 'script' of sorts, but whatever form of words you opt for, make sure you keep it relaxed and light. (You'll have noticed how this is a bit of a theme in successful sales.)

What you say might go like this:

> **YOU:** *Hi Roger, I understand that you're the person responsible for learning and development for the firm. Is that right?*
>
> **ROGER:** *Yes, I am.*
>
> **YOU:** *Thank goodness for that! Well, my name's Nick, Nick Davies, and I used to be a lawyer but turned away from the dark side some years ago and now spend my time travelling up and down the country teaching lawyers in a range of communication skills. The reason I'm calling is that I'd really like to pop in and see you, find out more about the firm, how you go about training your lawyers in those kinds of skills and to see whether what I do might be of help. I'm in London on the 4th and 5th and since you're the first person I've called, you can choose which one's best for you.*

Then *shut up* and wait for him to answer. Do not keep talking.

If the prospect asks you questions, then answer them, but *do not* go in to lots of detail and don't even *think* about 'selling' over the phone.

It takes 32 seconds to have that conversation – I've just timed it. Even though it's very quick, I want you to notice what I'm trying to get across in such a short time. Let's look at it point by point:

- I clarify that he is the right person to talk to.
- I introduce myself and repeat my first name.
- I give him an insight into my background and – in terms of teaching lawyers – increase my credibility. (Someone who used to be a lawyer has an insight into the profession.)
- I introduce some humour with 'dark side'. This works because many learning and development managers are former lawyers; even if they aren't, they do understand that working with them

50

brings some unique difficulties. It also shows that I'm not taking myself too seriously.

- 'Travelling up and down the country' – factually correct, but also signals that I am busy and probably have a lot of experience working with many different law firms.
- 'The reason I'm calling' – straight to the point.
- 'Find out about your firm and see whether what I do might be of help' – I am interested in finding out about what you do (so I'm not just coming along to tell you what I've got/do), but I am ultimately hoping that you might use my services – in other words, I am coming to sell to you, albeit in a very gentle, no-pressure kind of way.
- 'I'm in London on the 4th and 5th' – the alternative close, which I'll talk more about below. This also indicates that I intend to be busy enough to fill two days with appointments.
- 'You are the first person I've called' – I'm ringing a number of firms but someone's got to be first; again, just a little light humour. If I have other meetings arranged or am in the process of arranging them with other firms, then I will make a point of telling him the names of these organizations.

This 'script' works for me and although not every call I make is the same, I pretty much stick to it. You need to develop your own script, in the same way you develop your own style when writing a letter.

The point is to get a bit of your personality across in addition to telling the prospect why you want to meet up. It will take you a good few calls before you settle on a form of words you feel comfortable with, but it will happen – trust me.

Getting the commitment to a meeting

Before making the call, you *must* have three dates to offer: two close together and the third a few weeks later, in case the person is away on holiday or something. For the purposes of this example, we'll go for the 4th or 5th or the 23rd.

Do not ask: 'So, when would it be most convenient?' There are two reasons you should never do this:

- It hands control over to him (since it's Roger we're talking about). He is free to say any day he chooses: '17 April 2017 is good for me.' In that case you're stuffed.

- It makes it difficult for him to make a decision. Contrary to popular belief, we don't like too much choice, because when faced with limitless options we find it difficult to choose just one.

By offering Roger two alternatives, I am making it easy for him to choose. All he has to do is look at two adjacent pages on his diary, rather than trawl through umpteen of them.

This method of getting people to commit is known as the 'alternative close' in the sales world and is highly effective when you want to secure dates for meetings and appointments.

Of course, if Roger says he is out of the office on the 4th and 5th, then you can offer him the 23rd. *Don't be too available.* Don't ever say: 'Well, I'm free for the next three weeks' or 'I'm free pretty much any time that suits you.' Such phrases tell your caller that you aren't busy and may leave them thinking: 'He can't be that good, or he'd be busy.'

One of the things that makes people or objects desirable is scarcity. A few months after Ferrari launches a new model, secondhand Ferraris (sorry, 'previously enjoyed') are quite often more expensive than a new one. People don't want to wait six months to have a new car built and will pay over the odds to get one 'now'.

Let's say Roger picks the 5th. You then offer him another alternative:

YOU: *Morning or afternoon best for you?*

ROGER: *Morning would be better.*

You then move it on to pinning down a time, although you continue offering alternatives: '10.15 or 11.15?'

If someone suggests 10 am for a meeting, how long will the meeting last? An hour? 10.30 – half an hour? 10.15 – 15 minutes or 45 minutes?

We tend to block time into hours, so when I contact someone and suggest 10 am for a meeting, they will automatically block out until 11 in their diary. Why can't this meeting last until 10.25 or 10.40? It might well do, but that won't stop the person blocking out a full hour. If it does finish after 40 minutes, they will regard the meeting as having finished 'early'.

I like to set up meetings for 15 minutes past the hour because people will assume that it'll be over within 45 minutes, which it normally is; although you'd be amazed at how many do run on until quarter past the hour.

I know this seems silly, but it works and sends a strong, almost subliminal message to the person you want to see that you aren't going to waste their time (and, from their point of view, even if you did, you'd only have wasted 45 minutes of it rather than a whole hour).

The other benefit I get from this is that I tend to make sure I arrive outside the person's office or in the coffee shop on the hour, which gives me 15 minutes to wander about nearby in the case of the former, or to get myself a drink and get settled in the case of the latter.

If you have one or two appointments already
Remember when you are setting the meeting up to mention other firms and organizations you are in contact with: 'Mmm, let's see, I could do the 23rd because I'm in your neck of the woods on the 22nd seeing Felix at Stromberg and Emilio at Palmyra.' You get the picture.

This is for two reasons:

- Other people in your position in your sector think it's worth meeting me (the inference being: so you should as well).
- Credibility – if these people have agreed to see him then I might as well do the same.

I mention the names of individuals because there is a good chance that in a particular sector, in a particular city, people occupying the role of Head of Learning and Development will know each other and may have some kind of formal or informal network.

What if the prospect asks questions?

Once you have got through to your prospect, the chances are that he or she will ask questions. While you should answer these honestly and efficiently, you should *not* go into detail, because you'll end up selling over the phone and that's difficult and best avoided.

Here are some of the questions you may get asked and how you handle them.

> **QUESTION:** *Could you tell me what other services you offer?*
>
> **ANSWER:** *We offer a range of commercial legal services to clients, including mergers and acquisitions, financing, construction and employment. I'll be able to explain in more detail when we meet up. Is Tuesday or Wednesday better for you?*
>
> **QUESTION:** *Do you have experience of asset finance work in the shipping sector?*
>
> **ANSWER:** *We have a great deal of experience in many areas, including some shipping-related work. When we meet next week I'll be able to tell you more about what we do.*
>
> **QUESTION:** *Could you tell me what you charge?*

ANSWER: *It depends on what type of work we are undertaking and what level of service you require. That's the sort of thing we can have a natter about when we meet up. Is Monday morning or afternoon better for you?*

As you can see, you are acknowledging their question, while simultaneously avoiding going into detail and closing – the alternative close in your replies to the first and third questions, and the assumptive close in the second (more about closing later in the book).

Experience tells me that questions regarding price are those that people fear most. This needn't be the case. In fact, they should be cherished, because any enquiry regarding price is what is referred to as a 'buying sign'.

Someone with no interest whatsoever in purchasing your product doesn't care less what you charge. Whenever I've answered one of those calls offering me replacement windows, I have never asked how much they were charging – it's of no interest to me because I'm not in the market for new windows.

Questions about price – especially direct ones like 'How much do you charge?' – throw an awful lot of people off balance, whether they're asked over the phone or face to face. Indeed, us Brits can feel so awkward about cost that often even the person asking is a bit embarrassed to raise the matter.

Only today, I was in conversation with someone over the phone, talking about the possibility of me coming in to do some training for members of her team, when she said: 'Of course, we'll need to determine what your fee structure is to see whether it accords with our forthcoming budget projections for the coming year.'

We were getting on well, so I just said: 'You mean, how much do I charge?' She hesitated, before replying 'Yes'.

I want to highlight questions regarding how much you charge because you do not want to enter into discussions surrounding price over the phone or via email during the initial 'connecting' phase of the process, *especially when selling a service*. It's fine once you've got a bit of a relationship going or have done some work for one division of an organization and are now talking to someone in a different one.

Talking about price is a little less dangerous when you're selling a product, although not much – how do they know that your apple-based shampoo is the same as their current provider's, for example?

If you sell a service, then, as I have already mentioned, what you are really selling is you and a prospective customer or client has no idea what value they would put on 'you' until they've met you.

Be proud of your price. Don't apologise for what you charge. You wouldn't walk in to a Ferrari dealership, and hear a sales guy apologize for charging £150,000 for one of their cars, would you? Or saying: 'It's expensive isn't it and to be honest it's only got the two doors and is a bit tricky to get in and out of as well. A weekly shop's out of the question. Still, what with Tesco delivering nowadays . . .'

No, he'd get you to sit in it and start asking you questions, but mainly he'd just let you really savour the touch, smell and feel of the car.

Issues surrounding price should preferably be discussed face to face – as with all negotiation.

Here's a price enquiry I received and my reply, which may give you an idea how to deal with such questions.

> *Good morning Nick. Thanks for your introductory infor-mation – it's a real pleasure to read someone's 'blurb' and find yourself smiling!*
>
> *You've given me a very clear picture of who you are and what you're about – my immediate question is: 'If I were to engage your services how much would it cost me?'*

Given that you're based in Scotland but are in Bristol on Monday, if I feel your fees are within reach (I try and get everything I can for next to nothing as any good buyer does, whilst expecting the best quality!) I'd be happy to make time on Monday 11th to see you if that's OK with you?

I look forward to hearing from you. Sorry I haven't got time to call you instead of sending this email – I'm a victim of my diary this week I'm afraid.

Regards

Sue

My reply, via email:

Glad you like the blurb, Sue.

Talking about money via email is so horrid, isn't it? And if you think I can help you make your fee earners better at winning business and I think it would be lovely to work with you, then I don't think we would allow price to get in the way: it never has with any other client.

Let's meet up and have a natter about it.

However, you can rest assured that I am, as they say in the L'Oréal ads, 'worth it'.

Nick

Getting into a discussion about price over the phone with someone you have never met and who has never seen what you do is a waste of time, but doing it via email is even worse (there's no pitch, tone, pace, volume, intonation or emotion in an email).

If I'd given Sue a price via email she would have no way of knowing whether what I was selling was worth it. If I sell a product I can send her an example of it in the post, but I'm selling a service. While she can get an idea of what I cover by looking at my brochure or website, there's no substance to it: no flesh on the bones.

What if you detect reluctance?

Sometimes when you phone people out of the blue and try to arrange to see them, you detect hesitancy or reluctance in their voice during the conversation. You get the impression that they are asking you questions as a way of being polite because they really don't want to see you.

Should this be the case, then be sensitive to it. Don't roll over straight away – keep coming back to the dates when you can see them, as I've detailed above. However, if you sense that you have pushed it enough, take the initiative and therefore the pressure off the other person and say something along these lines:

> **YOU:** *Look, would be easier just to send you something in the post so you can get a better feel for what I do?*

What's amazing is that as soon as you say this they immediately relax, because you've articulated what they were thinking. Normally I get this kind of response:

> **ROGER:** *Oh, do you mind? That would be really helpful.*
> **YOU:** *Sure, that's no problem. I'll get that out to you today/tomorrow.*

Once you secure the meeting

If, after a brief chat to Roger, he agrees to meet you for a coffee, then thank him and let him know that you'll confirm by email. Something along these lines is nice:

> *Hi Roger, good to chat to you a moment ago and just to confirm that we are meeting up at 10.15 on Monday 5 August at Caffè Nero on Holborn, just by Chancery Lane tube. I look forward to seeing you then.*
> *Nick*

You should also send him some more information about what you do in the post in anticipation of your get-together, which you may or may not tell him you're going to send.

Sending information ahead of the meeting is always a wise move, because then the other person has a far better impression of what you do, and it gives them the opportunity to think of some questions.

If you wait until you meet to furnish your prospect with material, then at the end of the appointment she can fall back on: 'Well, I'll think about it once I've taken a look through your literature.'

Connecting by Email

Let me lay my cards on the table with regard to email. I don't rate it as a way of connecting with people with whom I want to secure a meeting, mainly because it doesn't often succeed.

How many emails fill your inbox every day? 50? 100? 200? How long does it take for one of those emails to be pushed so far down the list that the ones above drown it? How many emails that you know are sales emails do you open?

I get emails from organizations of which I am a very regular customer: British Airways, Flybe, Amex, Mercedes, Tesco, Bannatyne's Gym. These aren't from companies about which I know nothing or of which I've have never heard, never mind those trying to flog me stuff, or attempting to get to visit me and chat over a coffee... I don't open any of them because I'm too busy. And guess what? So are all the people you've been sending 'let me introduce myself' emails.

Email is too easy. It tells the prospective customer that you're just like everyone else out there attempting to win her custom: you can't be bothered.

If I really can't talk you out of using email, then either write your email like you would a letter (see below) or really pull the stops out and try something like this:

Good afternoon Geoff

I was happily minding my own business doing a load of training for all the partners at ABC a couple of months ago, when a bloke called John Smith comes up to me, tells some story about flogging his house to a Paul Scholes and then says, 'Next time you're in town I'll take you for a spot of lunch.'

So a few weeks later we do lunch and he says – as I have a mouthful of what he assures me is 'the most expensive sandwich in London' – that I should meet up with you because, and I quote, 'John at XYZ would love the kind of stuff that you've done for us and you'd get on like a house on fire.' He then proceeds to write your email address on my napkin and as he hands it to me, adds, 'Oh, and mention Sarah because she'd be interested in what you do as well.'

So that's why I've got in touch, Geoff. And while John suns himself on a boat off the coast of Majorca with his wife, the kids, the best client and the best client's mistress (you just could not make it up), I wonder if, when you are next in London, I might buy you a coffee and see if what he says is true.

Cheers

Nick

Nick Davies LLB. Hons. Barrister

LETG Trainer of the Year '07/08

That's a copy of an email I sent to the managing partner of one of Europe's largest professional services firms – cold (the names have been changed to protect the innocent).

Now, I don't know how many emails the managing partner of one of the world's largest professional services firms receives in a day, but I bet it's a lot. And I bet he's never got one like that.

What happened? His HR director contacted me (he'd forwarded the email to her), we met and I was asked to tender for a load of work.

I wasn't awarded the contract, but I got a hell of a lot further than the countless other people who sent emails like this:

> *Dear Sir*
>
> *I work for a global human resource strategic skills enhancement company that is accredited with ISO 4386 by . . .*

That's quite enough about email. Let's talk about letters.

Connecting by Letter

I love sending letters because they are a superb way to *CONNECT* with people and they are so very rarely sent in the age of electronic communication. They can really make an impact.

Letters are a major plank of my business development activity. I write them at every possible opportunity, because apart from standing up and speaking, they are the single most effective way of *CONNECTING* with people emotionally.

If you want to stand out and have a chance of winning business, then you *must* stop doing what all your competitors are doing and do something different.

Some wise person once said: 'They don't erect statues to critics.' Doing things differently is scary. Going out on a limb and taking a chance is potentially disastrous, but if you continue attempting to connect with potential clients in the same way that everyone else is, whether you win business becomes nothing more than a lottery.

You can write letters to people at any point in the business development process: when following up after networking, in response to the 'Will you send something in the post?' request, or prior to making a cold call if you've not been able to get through to anyone in the organization.

A letter is a superb way of getting across your personality; of providing an insight into your character and your attitude; in other words, of making an emotional connection.

Here is a typical letter I send. Read it and then I'll go through it in detail, because, while it's representative of what I'm like as a person, it does contain stuff that you should be putting in your letters, irrespective of your own style.

Hello Alison

My name's Nick and I run the Really Great Training Company.

I used to be a lawyer but I turned away from the 'dark side' some years ago and now, rather ironically but nevertheless appropriately, spend my time training and coaching lawyers at all levels, from countries across the globe, how to network, present, pitch, influence and develop business.

Although I live in Edinburgh most of my work is with firms in London – in fact, I suspect that I may be the only person in Scotland with an Oyster Card on automatic top-up! – doing work for firms such as Zorin, Auric, SpellBound & Dazed, TCR, HDT and a whole bunch of others.

I last spoke about training on a visit to your offices at 45 High Street, where I met Sally Brown, but that was 18 months ago and you were with a different firm and so was I. So what I'd dearly like to do now is pop in and see you, find out how you go about training and whether what I do might be of help.

I shall give you a bell in a week's time and see if we can put a date in the diary.
Regards
Nick

Let's pull this letter apart.

One rule to start off: one page of A4 only. Two pages are too fiddly and reading them is too much like hard work. If you can't fit it all on one side, then reduce your font to 10 (no smaller); if it still doesn't fit take some words out.

The paragraphs break down as follows:

1. A quick and friendly introduction.
2. Credibility – I was a lawyer, I work with lawyers all the time from all over the world and I'm busy.
3. Credibility – These are major players in your sector. If they use me, I'm probably worth meeting.
4. The background and the reason for contacting you.
5. What I'm going to do next and when.

The last point about letting them know what I'm going to do next and when is an important one. Remember, keeping control of the business development process is something you should be doing at all times.

Compliment Slips and Brochures

I don't have compliment slips. I have postcards with my details and logo on, with a nice blank section on which I can write a few lines. Compliment slips are boring, dull, a waste of print and paper, no one ever looks at them and the term 'With compliments' is antediluvian. If you have to have them, then substitute 'Thank you' for 'With compliments'.

And never, ever email out a brochure. Why? When was the last time you were sent a brochure via email and actually read it, all the way through? Put simply, people can't be bothered opening up brochures in Adobe Acrobat, particularly since it seems to be in constant need of updating.

Let me tell you how adamant I am about this: if someone asks me to email a copy of my brochure (some firms have strong environmental policies and are attempting to 'go paperless' and prefer electronic stuff), I send a real one *as well*. Us human beings do like having our senses stimulated – touch, sight, smell, sound, taste – and you only get one of those with an email but four with the real thing (I am assuming no one eats my printed matter).

I want people literally to get a 'feel' for what I do. My designer Simon and I spent hours and hours developing those few pages. I wrote the copy and he did the artwork. We sweated over layout, colours and even the type and quality of the paper we should use, because I wanted people to want to handle the brochure, open it and see what was inside.

If you don't have that kind of brochure in your organization, get marketing to sort it out. As far as I'm concerned, if your company information isn't engaging as well as informative, save yourself the cash and stop producing it. The person you send it to will just bin it anyway.

Speaking in Public

The sharp-eyed among you will have noted this little fella sitting unassumingly at the foot of the 'ways to connect with people' list at the start of this chapter, underneath 'Networking (at an event)'.

I'm not devoting more than a few lines to the huge subject of public speaking because that's what my next book is about, but I do want to tell you why it I believe it to be one of the best ways to make an emotional connection with your target market:

- I can't think of a better way to establish your credibility, experience, knowledge of subject and thus your trustworthiness to lots of people in a short period.

- If you make your talk or speech anything like half decent and make a connection with your audience, you'll stand out from everyone else who's putting the audience into a persistent vegetative state by reading their 36 slides.

- It beats the hell out of attending an event and having to wander around with your badge on, making friends with people. First because we tend to feel a bit awkward about it; and second because, with all the will in the world, you cannot possibly make a connection with everyone, whereas you can if you are speaking at the event.

- It works. I attend very few networking events. The last one was at Claridges in Mayfair, where there was me and 149 women. (I leave you to work out why I accepted the invitation.) However, I do speak at a number of events and conferences for free, and I *always* get work as a direct result of doing so.

On one occasion I had reached firm 16 on my top 20 list. I contacted the guy who headed up the training and development team and got an appointment to see him for a coffee. Although he was 16th on the list, I think he was possibly the 5th person I saw.

During our conversation he asked me if I had heard of the L.E.T.G. (Legal Education and Training Group). I said that I hadn't.

He went on to explain that it was an association made up of the heads of training and development at the principal law firms in the country. "Oh, that's interesting," I replied.

The conversation then continued thus:

ME: *Do you have an annual conference?*

HIM: *Yes, we do. It's in November.*

ME: *I'd really like to speak at that. How can I go about making that happen?*

HIM: *Mmm, that might be a possibility. Leave it with me and I'll have a word with a few people.*

I did speak at that conference. I wasn't one of the main speakers, I just ran one of four 'break-out' sessions that delegates could opt to hear and was persuaded to deliver an impromptu after-dinner speech for the delegates.

I can't begin to tell you how much business I got as a direct result of speaking at that conference. Here, yet again, is an example of sales people being lazy and working smarter rather than harder.

If you are not a confident speaker, go and get some coaching, then start speaking and get good at it. It's a very quick and effective way of connecting with people in your target market and it'll set you apart from your competitors, ensuring that you are remembered by your target audience.

Following Up

As part of covering how to connect with your targets, I have devoted a lot of pages to cold calling to ensure that I've covered all the bases and that you get a detailed idea of how to handle most situations.

Some of you will never need to cold call and you should be grateful for that, because going in cold is certainly the trickiest way of generating sales. It's just so much easier to sell more stuff to existing clients or to tackle those who can be introduced to you by someone else.

Still, there will be some of you who do have to do it and some of you who are just plain odd such as me – who cold call just for the thrill of it and to keep themselves sharp.

I confess to doing one or two cold calls a month, just to make sure that I can still do it. I also find it the biggest thrill in sales: contacting someone cold, getting them to agree to see you, meeting them and then a few months later they become a client. Something from absolutely nothing: it's a real buzz! I reckon the day I can no longer do this is the day I'll jack in selling.

We've also had a good look at the not-so-humble letter as well as the ubiquitous and so easily deleted email. I hope you can see what a really powerful emotional connection it's possible to make through a letter. Not only does it allow you to let your character and personality flood out, but the mere fact you've been bothered to type it, print it, put it in an envelope and address it, and (unless you work in a large organization) put a stamp on it and take it to a post box, shows that you have gone to some effort. You haven't run a marathon, but you might as well have compared to everyone else who's attempted to win that person's business.

While most organizations proudly proclaim on their website that they 'offer a personal service and are different to all their competitors', you demonstrate it. You aren't caring by saying you care, you do it by showing that you do.

Whether you opt to connect with someone over the phone – and you speak to them or leave a message on their voicemail – or send a letter or an email, you must also *FOLLOW UP* after each one. Sure, there will be exceptions, like that s**t-or-bust cold email to the managing partner of a professional services firm, but they should be just that – exceptions.

Following up is all about keeping in control and you do this by ending your emails, phone calls/voicemails and letters by telling the person what you're going to do next and when you're going to do it.

Never end any kind of contact with: 'So, if there is anything else I can help you with, please don't hesitate to call.'

Chapter 5

NETWORKING

BUSINESS TALK FOR 'GETTING ON WITH PEOPLE'

A t the start of the previous chapter I listed networking as one of the ways in which you could make an emotional connection with prospective clients. However, it's such a large subject, one that almost stands alone because it has become such an integral part of most working people's lives, that it warrants its own chapter.

Most of us are not keen at networking, which is a pity, because it's a great way to *CONNECT* with *and* move on to the third stage of my business development model, *MEET* people.

What Is Networking?

When most people think about networking they conjure up a room full of strangers, with name badges, clutching a glass of Pinot while balancing a plate of nibbles, desperately worried about breaking into a group of people and indulging in conversation, anxious that they need to appear both interested and interesting. Such events may be external to your place of work, where you are the guest. Others are perhaps in-house, where you and colleagues are acting as hosts to people you have invited.

I would also include in networking those conversations you may strike up with complete strangers on a train, plane or in a waiting room. However, as I always explain to people new to the commercial world (such as recent graduates), 'networking' is just the term people in business give to 'getting on with people'.

What I don't cover here is social networking. Technology has given us a whole host of ways of getting and keeping in touch, but the bottom line remains that people do business with people they have met and if I want to meet people, I still prefer the phone.

Don't be fooled into thinking that because you are connected to perhaps tens or even hundreds of people, you have a relationship with them, let alone one that would lead to business. In order to achieve that, you have to go and see them. LinkedIn, along with every other networking site, is simply a step or a conduit to getting to *MEET* up with someone.

Overall, I have to say that people who are serious about developing business are out there, making the calls, meeting people and, more importantly, making money. In other words, they're far too busy to have the time to tell the rest of the world how busy they are or to whom they have just 'connected'.

Networking with Strangers

I'm quite a chatty, friendly bloke. Not all the time: I can be a grumpy, miserable, antisocial so-and-so sometimes. However, I'm continually chatting to people I meet when I'm out and about. Ordinarily a brief exchange of words is all that occurs; however, on occasion the time, place and circumstances mean that a full-blown conversation ensues.

I'm fascinated by what people do with their time, whether that's in paid employment or otherwise, so I tend to listen with interest as the person tells me all about their job, their life, family and background. Normally, if I show a genuine interest in them, they tend to ask about what I do.

Most people are interested to learn what I do for a living and the story of how I got there. What is more, occasionally but only occasionally, they will go further and ask me for a business card and make some remark about either a colleague or a friend possibly being interested in using my services. If that is the case, then I hand over my card – no more than that.

The point is, always keep your ears and eyes open, because you never know where business will spring from.

The Networking 'Event'

Let's look in more detail at how you handle a more formal, organized networking occasion: how do you prevent it being little more than a colossal waste of time?

Go to the Right Events

People starting out in business have a habit of joining generic networking groups: the kind where you turn up every week, have to do a little speech about what your business does and furnish another member with the name of a lead. While I'm sure these are lovely social get-togethers filled with bonhomie, you don't get professional sales people going to them (for very long). They are a waste of time because they are full of people just starting up their own business, all of whom share two things in common: they haven't got any money and they don't know anyone. If they did, they wouldn't be there.

It's my experience that at this kind of event you always meet a printer, an independent financial adviser, a 'life coach', a mortgage broker, a computer repair person, assorted designers – graphic, web, soft furnishings and interior – a trainee accountant, a trainee lawyer, a personal trainer and the obligatory weirdo with a half-brained idea that no one, not even his mum, is going to buy into.

I want to target the legal market, so guess what? I go to events where there are wads of lawyers and/or the training and development managers of law firms. I could attend events where there are people from the hospitality industry, because they could buy my services as well, but that's not my focus.

You do not have the luxury of wasting your time – especially in the early days of developing business – by attending the wrong events. If you're unsure which events to go to, just ask yourself whether the people there are in your *HOT*, *WARM*, *TEPID* or *COLD* market – the warmer the better.

Only go to events where you know there are going to be people from the sectors you want to get into or that you sell to already. I think the term used in the movie *Top Gun* is 'a target-rich environment'.

This is why doing your targeting is so important. Too many people waste time, attending 'general' events in the hope that they will bump into people who will want to buy or based on the mistaken belief that they can sell what they have to anyone and everyone.

Events You Are Hosting

If you have invited clients or prospective clients to a venue (either at your offices or elsewhere), then you can't leave who meets who to chance. You have to play the part of a host, as you would in your home, where you would give thought and consideration to who you'd sit together, based on your assessment of who'd get on best with one another.

So, when deciding who to invite to this event, think about the following:

- You must speak to your existing clients (remember, they need to know that you still love them).
- Who else in your team or department should meet a particular client?
- Who in your client's team would you like to chat to?

- Which people outside of your team or department would you like them to meet? (This is where cross-selling starts and ensures that the client doesn't think that you only offer employment law.)

- Do you have any clients with whom you think your other clients would get on? (This is a cracker, because if you can introduce two clients who end up doing business with one another, they will both love you to bits.)

The large law firm I worked for hosted many client events. They usually took the form of seminars aimed at updating clients with the latest developments in law, but they had quite a social slant to them, with drinks and nibbles never far away.

I attended one such event hosted by the Employment Department at Old Trafford, where the event organizers did something that worked really well in getting people to mix. Each delegate's name badge had a coloured spot on it: blue, purple, red etc. When they were given their badge at registration, a member of the law firm's events team would walk them over to the table where other people wearing the same colour had been shown. So we ended up with 'purple', 'blue', 'red', 'orange', 'green' tables and so on, around which were a nice mix of individuals whom the firm thought would get on well together.

Incidentally, if you are running seminars, make sure they are superb. You want people to be leaving your event saying that it was the best seminar they've ever been to and that they can't wait to come to the next one.

Events at Which You Are a Guest

Once you know which sectors you are going after, find out whether there is a trade association or professional body that holds regional events, or has an annual conference or exhibition, and go to those events.

Prior to the event

Contact the organizer and ask for a delegate list so that you can see whether people from the sectors you're interested in are attending. If they say they can't give out a delegates list because of data protection, thank them for their time and then contact someone else involved in organizing the event who actually knows what they're talking about.

Assuming you get hold of a list – and most of the time you will – then take a look at it and find the names of anyone you know already who's going. Contact them and check if they still intend to be there.

This is a good thing to do, because there is nothing worse than walking into a networking event not knowing anyone and then having to strike up conversation with strangers. While it's dumb to spend all evening chatting to someone you know already, knowing that there will be someone there that you can have as your first point of contact can be reassuring to many people.

Another advantage of hooking up with someone you know is that they may be able to introduce you to people they know but you don't.

Who do you talk to?

If you have arrived with someone start by talking to them (it would be rude not to).

However, in circumstances where you haven't, take a look at the delegate list and see whether there is the name of someone you'd particularly like to talk to. Then while you're still at the registration point you can ask the organizers whether that person has arrived and, if so, would it be possible to point them out.

I have been on the receiving end of this and it's quite flattering when someone you don't know approaches you and says: 'Hi, you must be Nick Davies. My name's Max Kalber. I hope you don't mind me introducing myself to you, but I really wanted to meet you and have a chat.'

What is more, it delays the point at which I have to look around the room for someone to talk to and that can only be good because, if you're anything like me, that's always the awkward bit.

Getting conversations going

You have arrived at registration and pinned your badge on. On behalf of blokes everywhere, I implore all women to pin your badge high up on your lapel or blouse, anywhere but on your chest. It's really embarrassing for a man to try to see your name and that of the organization you represent, when the manoeuvre involves having to look directly at either your left or right boob. You wouldn't like it if we wore our badges on the fly of our trousers – not nice at all.

Go to the area where the drinks are. Invariably this is tea or coffee. Pour yourself a cup. Nine times out of ten, another delegate will approach the table in anticipation of pouring themselves a drink once you've done. Look towards them and ask: 'Are you having coffee?' If they answer 'Yes', then give them the one you have just poured. Or, if they've poured theirs already and are waiting for you to finish with the milk, ask them if they'd like milk. If 'Yes', pour it for them.

This works with any liquid. I don't want you reading this book only to go away thinking: 'Nick seemed to be quite specific about coffee and milk, but what about tea? I don't drink coffee or take milk! Oh no, maybe this is why I struggle at networking events?'

I use this natural ice-breaker all the time because it's relaxed, perfectly natural and really easy to do, not to mention very effective. When I was director of a recruitment firm I did this and got talking to someone who turned out to be a fantastic recruitment consultant with a rival agency. Six weeks later they were working for us and bringing in loads of cash – all from a simple 'Would you like coffee?'

It also works because it brings in a little bit of psychology concerning reciprocity. If you give someone something for free, without being asked, they feel obliged to give you something in return – in this scenario, that's time.

Imagine if you arrived at the drinks table at a networking event, were offered a cup off coffee that someone had poured for themselves and you just said 'Thanks' and walked away. It would be hard to do, wouldn't it? It's impolite. In fact it's only happened to me once.

The drink offer only works assuming that you are neither the first nor the last person arriving at the event. If the former, then you'd have to hover around the drinks table and end up looking a bit like a waiter. If the latter, you'd have to shout across the room to ask if anyone would like a top-up. This is contrived and makes you appear weird.

Moving in

What if you've got no one to talk to when you walk into the event, no one is able to introduce you to someone and no opportunity has arisen at the drinks table?

First, you need to make an assessment of the room. You've been doing this every time you've been to an event, it's just that you might not be aware you were doing it.

There may be a couple of large groups of individuals gathered together. There are a number of smaller groups of three or four people. Then there are a number of 'couples' and, of course, people like you, who are on their own.

Groups of four or more are hard to break into. I don't bother: it's too difficult and too awkward. However, if it's your only choice, then approach the group so that you are facing the person speaking and make eye contact with them, so that they in turn acknowledge you.

Groups of three or four are easier than the big groups, but you still need to approach with caution. The first thing to do is to size these groups up. If from the body language and position of each person or from their conversation – assuming you can hear it – it would appear that they are work colleagues, deep in conversation, leave them to it. Even if these people are not from the same firm, they may be continuing a conversation that began in the taxi on the way to the event.

On the other hand, if you get the feeling they are not colleagues and the body language would suggest that this is a relaxed, informal group, then approach and ask if you can join them.

This does rely on you being assertive and probably taking a deep breath before making a move, but if the alternative is standing on your own all evening feeling like a clown at a funeral, then you've everything to gain – including keeping your dignity.

People in twos are easier to approach, although once again you must make an assessment based on their respective body language and position relative to one another. If they are close and there's touching, it's perhaps prudent to leave them to it. Otherwise twos are often, at least subconsciously, looking for a third person to join them and you can clearly see this in the way they are standing.

Very often you'll see two people at 'ten to two' next to each other, as though waiting for someone to complete the triumvirate. Be aware of this – you'll be amazed at how many times you witness it. It's an invitation for someone to join them, so accept it.

What about people on their own? Have you ever been stood on your own at an event? How do you feel if someone comes up and talks to you? Exactly: relieved.

People alone are the easiest to talk to. They are in exactly the same boat as you. They feel awkward and shy about making an approach. They obviously know no one and are worried about being the only person without a 'friend', thus giving the impression to others that they must be in some way odd.

To sum up: the coffee/tea ploy works a treat. If that's not viable, go and speak to someone who's on their own.

Alcohol

Quite often when I'm talking to young professionals, the subject of alcohol comes up. More than a few delegates will express concern at the prospect of becoming a little drunk and saying the wrong thing to the wrong person or behaving inappropriately. They want my advice on what to do in such situations.

I have to confess that the first time this matter was raised, I was dumbstruck, because it seems patently obvious to me – and quite likely to lots of you reading this – that you *don't drink alcohol* or just have one and then don't have any more.

If you are new to the professional or business world, I cannot stress enough just how important this is. If you drink too much you lose control of what you are doing and what you're saying. Even if senior managers don't take you to one side and mention it, either at the time or later, make no mistake about it, they will have clocked it and, in all likelihood, told other senior people, including those within the personnel department. All of that will affect your future career advancement, and the first thing you'll know is your head hitting a glass ceiling or, even more subtle, your feet being affixed to a sticky floor.

Food

Food is another subject that can create anxiety. People say things like: 'It's so awkward when you have a glass in one hand and a plate of food in the other and you're attempting to have a conversation with someone. What on earth do you do? I always feel so self-conscious.'

When you think about this it's quite simple: put the plate down and finish what's in your mouth, then you can talk.

Remembering names

Are you any good at remembering names?

Yeah, I thought not. Neither am I, although I'm better than I was.

The first thing to note is that you don't *forget* the names of people you meet. It's simply that you don't hear them in the first place.

When two people meet for the first time they move through three initial steps of body language we're going to talk about later in the chapter: eye to body, eye to eye and then hand to hand. During this process, there is what is referred to as 'visual noise'. So when the person tells you their name, you're kind of deaf to it, which explains why after only three seconds you are looking at them and thinking: 'I have absolutely no idea what you are called and yet I know for a fact that you did tell me.'

If you're at an event where people are wearing name badges, this isn't too much of a problem, other than having to contort yourself to read the name clearly. But what do you do if there isn't a name badge?

Once you know that visual noise is happening, the next time someone introduces themselves to you or you are introduced to them, you repeat their name as soon as they have said it:

ME: *Hi, my name's Nick.*
PIERCE: *Hi, I'm Pierce.*
ME: *Hi Pierce, pleased to meet you.*

Then you use their name two or three times during the first minute and in that way you 'cement' it in your memory.

If you fail to do this, then you can always ask them to repeat it: 'Do you know, I'm terrible at names, what's yours again? I didn't quite catch it, I'm afraid.'

If someone asks you that how do you feel? Offended? Cut to the quick? Of course not! And neither will anyone you have to ask. In fact I would suggest that asking the person to repeat their name sends a very strong signal that their name is important to you.

You can only ask this once – and never of a long-term partner, it would really upset them . . .

Awkward and seemingly unpronounceable names

Don't struggle when you meet someone with an unusual name and certainly don't spend time talking to them without using their name. It's obvious to both parties when this is happening and it's really awkward if someone joins the conversation, looks to you for an introduction and you have no idea what to say.

If someone with an unusual name introduces themselves and you didn't get the pronunciation straight off, ask them to pronounce it again for you. They won't mind. They are used to people struggling with their name: they've experienced it all their life.

What I have found is that they are more than happy to help you get the pronunciation right and are chuffed that you've been one of the few people to take the time to get it right.

The Seven Stages of Body Language

I said earlier I was going to talk about body language, a subject that has always fascinated me. When you can read it, it makes you better at getting things off to a good start.

Research done by Desmond Morris, the anthropologist and author of the famous 1970s book *The Naked Ape*, demonstrated that when two human beings meet and get to know each other, they move through various stages of body language:

1. Eye to body.
2. Eye to eye.
3. Hand to hand.
4. Hand to shoulder.
5. Hand to waist.
6. Face to face.
7. Hand to head.

1. Eye to Body

Like it or not, the fact is that we make judgements about people as soon as we set eyes on them.

Those of you who have had cause to interview people will know this to be the case. You read someone's CV, like the sound of them and invite them in for an interview. Reception calls to let you know your interviewee has arrived. You turn up, the receptionist points them out and before they have even got up from the chair, you have formed an impression of them. And I'll bet there have been times when you've thought: 'You aren't getting the job, no matter how good you are. You might as well leave now!'

Once that initial impression is made we look for clues and signals that either support or run contrary to it. However, after the first couple of minutes, it's pretty much set and it's almost impossible for the person to convince you otherwise.

So it's pretty important that you look the part. A general rule of thumb is to be a little smarter than you think you should. If you're too scruffy it's difficult to dress things up, but if you're too smart you can simply remove your tie or jacket or undo a top button to create a more relaxed appearance.

Once again, it's about establishing trust and credibility. And let's be honest, if you can't dress yourself properly then you're making it difficult for yourself to establish either of these, particularly the latter.

2. Eye to Eye

We tend not to trust people who don't look us in the eye; we regard them as 'shifty'. Equally, you don't want to be staring at people, so look into their eyes and around their face. The vast majority of us look at a person's mouth when they are talking to us, which is fine, just don't neglect the eyes. And for goodness' sake, don't look over someone's shoulder when they are speaking to you: it's really off-putting.

3. Hand to Hand

We don't 'do' touching in our society. Walk down a busy high street or get on public transport and see how much effort we go to avoid touching each other. In such a culture, the handshake takes on a whole new significance.

Think about it. We only touch the hands of people we care deeply about: mum and dad when we were little, our kids if they are little, or our partner. Getting hold of another person's hand is a pretty intimate thing to do, so you'd better ensure your handshake is a decent one – dry, firm and complete. So much information is conveyed in that handshake.

Sweaty hands are a big 'no'! Before you go into a meeting, have an interview or embark on some networking, go and wash your hands – always!

Your handshake should be firm. A light, fluffy handshake says uncon-fident, not sure of yourself, perhaps sly, can't be bothered. But don't be bone-crunching, which is unnecessary and tends to be confined to those who are of a certain age, overpowering, trying to prove some-thing. That applies to women too: men notice women who have a decent, firm handshake.

Credibility is something that is established right from the start of a relationship; right from that very first encounter. A firm handshake, while looking someone in the eye, introducing yourself and saying 'Very pleased to meet you', is a superb way of establishing your cred-ibility and parity with them, right from the off – no messing or ambiguity.

There are four more stages of body language, but they get a bit rude and one, I don't know you well enough; and two, you really shouldn't be going past step three in most of your networking encounters!

To Kiss or Not to Kiss?

As the great Bob Dylan once sang: 'Times they are a changin'.'

People in Europe love a bit of cheek action – blokes and women alike – but us Brits are not too sure about it, particularly in a business setting.

Here's what I've observed travelling up and down the country.

- Men in business do not kiss each other.
- Women in business do not kiss each other – unless they know each other really well.
- Women in London kiss each other – one kiss on each cheek, but only when they know one another well.
- Women in London will kiss a bloke they know well – once on each cheek.
- When I'm in London and I meet a woman in London and I know her well, then I'll kiss her on both cheeks.
- When I meet a woman outside of London whom I know well, I'll kiss her on just one cheek.
- With men and women whom I don't know well or have never met before, I shake hands.

However, in the case of female clients, there does come a point when the relationship has moved from handshake to kiss, in which case I tend to shake their hand and give them a kiss. Once I know them better, I dispense with the handshake and just do the kiss (one cheek outside London, both cheeks in London).

If I meet a woman in London whom I know is based in an office outside London, then I just kiss the one cheek. The geographical location of the kissee is not important; rather, it is where she comes from.

Having said that, it still leaves you with the worry of when you feel a business relationship with a woman has moved to a level of familiarity where a kiss would not be inappropriate. This is a question to which there is no answer – you just have to play it by ear. If it feels right then go for it, but for heaven's sake be positive about it; don't mess about. There's nothing more guaranteed to make a woman's skin crawl than to have a bloke timidly, hesitantly, awkwardly plant a kiss on her cheek – no matter how well intentioned. And don't linger! Give her a kiss and back off.

If in doubt, don't kiss – no matter how well you know one another in a business context. If you feel awkward about it then you'll pass those uncertain feelings on to her.

Irrespective of how you have ended up exchanging names, kissing or shaking the hand of the person with whom you now find yourself talking, one thing's for sure: you'll have to chat about something and that's what I discuss in the next chapter.

Following Up

Very few people like networking, although most tend to enjoy it once they get into it and strike up a conversation with someone.

Make sure that you are going to the right events for you and spending miles more time listening rather than talking: you learn more, you don't have to be fascinating and people will think you're lovely.

Be aware of what you are saying even when you're not talking and get the touchy-feely bits right, whether that be the handshake or the kiss.

Above all, relax. Too many people put too much pressure on themselves to make as many high-level, potentially productive contacts as they can and tell them all about the marvellous services or products they offer. Networking events are about chatting to people and establishing the emotional connection that will make arranging to meet for a coffee (*FOLLOW UP*) dead easy and no big deal.

CHAPTER 6

SMALL TALK

THE SEEMINGLY MUNDANE ACTIVITY THAT MAKES A HUGE DIFFERENCE

The subject of what to talk about, whether at an event or at the start of a meeting, is of concern to a great many people. Confidence about small talk will stand you in good stead in both the networking and meeting phases of your business development activity.

When we meet someone for the first time we begin to establish a relationship by indulging in an activity known as 'self-disclosure'. We do this via what we all know as small talk or chit-chat.

Those in business often knock such talk as frivolous nonsense. They worry that they won't be taken seriously or regarded as professional if they aren't keeping the conversation to matters of business, which is why all too often I'll hear people start up a conversation with something like: 'So, how's business?' Or (one that I have heard a few times of late): 'So, what's keeping you awake at night?'

The first is hackneyed as an opener and the second just warrants a reply along the lines of: 'Well, I think my partner's having it off with the Eco-box delivery guy and my youngest has expressed an interest in banking.'

Topics

Interestingly enough, the topics regarded as suitable for small talk depend on where in the world you live. Given this book is for the UK market and that's the country I was born in and live in, I'll stick to that. In the UK it's OK to talk about:

- The weather
- Travel
- Holidays
- Sport (generally favoured by men, although not exclusively: my missus is a huge Leeds United fan and loves competitive sport – she's got trophies to prove it)
- Kids (dull if you haven't got them, but superb if you have)
- What you did/are doing at the weekend

The Weather

There are societies and cultures in which being polite is an overt, active thing. North America is one such society.

An American you have never met before will be quite happy to walk up to you and introduce himself to you with a hearty handshake and something like: 'Hi, my name's Hank, I'm from New York. It's the greatest city in the world.' (I met someone who had this said to them!)

Now, for someone from Great Britain, that's too much information, too soon and, dare I say, a tad presumptuous. We can get chatting to someone and talk to them for half an hour before saying 'I'm sorry, I didn't quite catch your name', in the full knowledge that we both know neither of us has told the other our name.

The reason is that in our society, being polite means not imposing ourselves on others – leaving them to themselves, respecting their privacy – which is why we have, over the years, come up with techniques to initiate conversations that do not make either of us feel uncomfortable, such as making some comment about the weather.

The reason the weather is such a good subject in the UK is, first, that it varies a great deal; secondly, we all experience it; and thirdly, it's a

89

great leveller. In a society that is still largely founded in the class system, the weather transcends all social divides. No matter how old or young you are, how little or how much money you earn, where you were educated or brought up, the weather is something we can all chat about. In fact, Kate Fox in her superb book *Watching the English* devotes a fascinating chapter to it. As an Englishman who's lived in Scotland since 2000 but who travels throughout the UK for work, I can say it is as applicable to the Scots, Welsh and Northern Irish as it is to the English.

Don't get me wrong: you can't spend 25 minutes talking to someone about the weather – unless, of course, your target market is meteorologists, in which case dive in!

Travel

For some reason we are obsessed with finding out how people we meet travelled to that location. We want to know and compare routes and modes of transport, and share travel horror stories with one another. The conversation often goes something like this:

'How did you get here today?'

'Oh, I got the tube.'

'Really, where did you get off?'

'Holborn.'

'Oh yes. I suppose Chancery Lane is a bit closer but Holborn's somehow easier, isn't it?'

'Do you take the Central Line for work?'

'Yes, but I normally get off at Bank and walk over London Bridge.'

'Really, so where do you come in from?'

'Liverpool Street, because I live just outside St Albans. Well, to be fair, it's more like Watford, but you know what I mean.'

*'Yes, so you work south of the river then. Isn't there a
train direct to London Bridge from where you are?'*
*'Well, yes, but it would mean catching a slightly earlier
train from St Albans and then changing at Blackfriars.
I refuse to leave the house before 6.30 am.'*
*'I know what you mean. I seem to spend my entire life
commuting.'*

If the weather has disrupted the travel system, then we are in small talk heaven! As Kate Fox observes in her wonderful book, we actually like moaning and use it to bond – so don't knock it.

That said, you don't want to be one of those dreary, pessimistic networkers whom everyone attempts to ditch as soon as they can. For some the glass isn't just half empty, it's cracked and the water's stagnant!

Sport

People love talking about their pastimes, passions and hobbies, particularly sport. You may worry that you don't know much about sport, but in fact you don't need to.

I don't play golf or rugby, but I meet loads of blokes who do and have and I can still have a conversation with them. I've picked up enough stuff about golf to be able to ask questions, which is great, because it takes the pressure off me to be interesting and I get to know more about the other person.

So, I ask them what they play off (their handicap), what club they belong to, which is their favourite course and which course they would play if they could pick any one in the world. And each time I get answers to these questions I learn more about golf for the next time I meet a golfer.

The same works for rugby or football: Which team do you support? How long have you supported them? Do you get to go to the matches?

How are you doing this season? Who's the best player right now? And so on.

If you want to know a little of what's going on, then all you need do is glance through the back pages of the *Metro* on your way to work, which will tell you who scored how many against whom the day before.

I'm not going to go through all the other topics for small talk, I simply wanted to point out how we use conversation to build rapport, and to learn more about one another – self-disclosure. These introductory subjects of small talk – travel, holidays, the weather and good old footie for the majority of blokes – lead inevitably on to other subjects, such as where we live, whether we have kids, where we went to school or university and what we do at the weekends. It's information that you glean by indulging in this kind of talk that is invaluable.

It's where we find common ground, see if we have shared values, and it's where we establish and build rapport: we discover whether the person with whom we are talking is like us. This is important, because people tend to buy from people they like and they like people like themselves.

Talking about Yourself

The information you learn during small talk will help you remember the person long after you've parted company, but it's also what *you* reveal that will enable them to remember you among all the other people they may have met over the previous few weeks.

I want you to be honest with yourself for a moment. If you and I met and got chatting at a networking event and you told me what you did and what your job title was, and I wasn't from the same industry or sector as you, would it mean anything to me and how long would it be before I forgot what you'd said?

When I was a lawyer I worked in the 'Commercial Dispute Resolution' department and specialized in contentious health, safety and environmental matters. (Oh, how the winter nights just flew by at my house!) Saying this to another lawyer or someone who worked within a law firm would be OK, because they could 'place' me and ask relevant questions to learn more. But if you know nothing about law the information would be utterly meaningless and, more importantly, completely forgettable. If networking is about making an impression and being remembered, then you would have failed.

Some years ago I arrived at a hotel in Derby, where I had been booked to talk to 70 trainee lawyers about networking skills. Before I did my bit, I got chatting to the senior partner of the large, national firm with which these delegates were going to work.

This guy was very well presented, exceptionally well spoken and by any objective standard what the vast majority of us would call seriously posh. Not so much a plum in his mouth but the entire orchard, complete with pickers from former Soviet states.

We did the handshake and pleased to meet you bit and fell in to easy conversation about *Casino Royale* (the film had recently been released), the role of Daniel Craig in comparison to previous Bonds, the way the director had interpreted the book and so on. I then made some comment regarding this guy's footwear, which resulted in a conversation about men's shoes, tailoring and suiting.

There was a natural pause in the conversation and I remarked to him that all we'd done for 20 minutes was indulge in small talk. I explained that one of the things I was going to talk to the 70 trainees about was this very subject – the importance of this kind of chit-chat.

He paused for a moment and looked thoughtfully before saying: 'Do you know, I don't think I've ever won a piece of work based on my technical ability as a lawyer; not one. I've won clients because I play tennis, because I have an interest in men's fashion and because I have a house in the South of France, but never solely on my knowledge of the law.'

His observation reflects what all those who earn their living in sales can attest to. Customers and clients buy things from and deal with people they like.

A final point about small talk: it shows that you're human and that you're in possession of a personality.

Are you a senior civil servant, an HR professional, an actuary, an investment manager, local government worker or accountant? Good: I've got a preconceived idea about all of those jobs – and so has every person you meet.

If you play a pivotal role in deciding housing policy for your local authority, then when we meet you at an event and you tell us that you're in local government, we all have a ready-made, off-the-shelf, nicely prejudiced view of what kind of person you are. Yep, people regard those in local government as scruffy, lazy – all on flexi-time – and incapable of making a decision without going through five committees, having a vote and then thinking about it for five months because not all the 'stakeholders' have been consulted fully. Oh, and you all have the obligatory four weeks' sick leave a year.

That's absolutely unfair, yet you need to be aware of how what you do and the sector in which you work are viewed by other people. If you are an accountant and you know that the rest of us think you are dull, anal and badly dressed, make sure that when people meet you they are pleasantly surprised – and that you don't conform to their stereotype.

I've mentioned already that not everyone you meet while out and about is going to end up being a client; and that this doesn't matter. What absolutely, positively and most definitely does matter is that when you part company, they come away with a favourable impression of you, as someone whose company they really enjoyed. You may not be mates for life, but they should feel that they've met a genuinely nice person.

As Sir Digby, now Lord Jones, former chairman of the CBI, said: 'Contrary to popular belief, genuinely, nice, honest, decent people actually do rather well in business.'

If you are an estate agent (no one has a preconceived idea of what they're like, do they?), you get chatting to someone and then move on after 20 minutes, you might not necessarily end up getting an instruction to buy or sell a house from them, but if back in their office a colleague asks how the networking event went last night and they can say, 'Do you know, I met a really nice woman last night who was an estate agent. We had a good chat. It turns out that she does X as a hobby and that she used to . . .', then that's a good result. You left a favourable impression, you blew away their preconceived image of estate agents and you raised your profile.

Being Memorable

One of the single biggest benefits to networking only within the markets you have targeted is that each time you attend a relevant event you raise your profile. This is why you should always try to speak at events: standing up in front of your target market is the best way to stand out and be remembered.

The sector you're in is probably no different to mine: awash with providers. There are countless firms offering training and coaching to every sector you can think of. So it's vital to stand out, and that starts with when you meet people.

There are plenty of ways to stand out and be remembered, but what we are talking about here is ways that are appropriate.

A former colleague of mine was at a breakfast networking event, organized by a large, international law firm's Glasgow office. There she was, buck's fizz in one hand and smoked salmon nibble in the other, chatting away to the managing partner and the director of communications, when she became aware of a bloke hovering just outside the cosy triumvirate. A moment later, he barged in to the group, pointed at my colleague's watch (a Rolex) and shouted: 'Is that real?'

Rather taken aback by the unsolicited intrusion, she replied: 'Yes, it is.'

'So's mine!' the response came back.

Of course the people she was talking to were rendered speechless by what they had just witnessed, although they managed to continue their conversation. This guy can certainly claim to have stood out at the event, but not for the right reasons.

Standing out is about being remembered for your personality or for your clothing – maybe you have a reputation for wearing funky shirts, great ties, perhaps it's your love of shoes or handbags. Maybe you are always the life and soul of the party? Perhaps you are the marathon runner within the office, or the sailor or the campanologist (look it up), or maybe you're the only person who ever thanks customers and clients for their business or sends flowers or cards to organizers of events and admin people working behind the scenes, who almost always get overlooked?

You need a 'story', a few 'highlights', a few little snippets that make you easy to remember – for the right reasons.

The best way to illustrate what I mean is by sharing with you what I know people remember about me.

First of all, I'm 6 feet 3 inches tall, have a Mancunian accent and wear glasses, so there are certain physical attributes that people recall. Aside from the physical stuff, there's also my work history and my hobbies.

My clients are the learning and development managers of law firms and they talk to each other, at their annual conference but also via email and phone. They ask each other's advice: 'Who do you use for this sort of training?' 'We're contemplating using this person for this subject; do you know anything about them?'

One of my clients might say, 'Yeah, we use Nick Davies,' to which the other person says, 'Oh, I have heard the name somewhere but I've never met him, although I'm sure Sean at Universal Exports was talking about him a few weeks ago.'

My client might reply: 'Yeah, he's that tall bloke from Manchester who used to be a lawyer. He's got a thing about shoes, wears funky shirts, does a bit of stand-up comedy.'

'Oh, yes, I know who you mean. I think Holly at Moonraker Inc. has used him recently. Have you got his number?'

Make sure people are talking about you and recommending you rather than your competitors! Stand out! Doing a good job is a given, so be remembered for other things.

Here's another one of those quotes:

> *My biggest mistake, the one for which I can never forgive myself, is that one day I ceased my obsessive pursuit of my own individuality.*
>
> *Oscar Wilde*

Write It Down

One last thing about small talk: write it down. Not all of the stuff you've heard and not while the person is talking to you, but make sure that afterwards – maybe while sitting in the car just before you leave the venue, on the train home or even next day in the office – you write down, on their business card, the salient points.

Start with the date and place you met them – it's amazing how quickly you'll forget. Then note stuff that's personal to them, such as where they are going on holiday, what football team they support, how many kids they have and their ages, any big event coming up like a wedding or weekend away, what they used to do for a living, where they hail from originally.

Even better, if your organization has some kind of client relationship system (CRM), then put all you know onto that.

All of this information is not there in order for you to embark on a campaign of quality stalking, but so that in three months' time, when you look back at your contacts, you'll be able to place that person and use some snippet of information to help make the *FOLLOW UP* call a whole lot easier. You'll be able to *CONNECT* with them, as I will illustrate later on.

Business Talk

Following on from the chit-chat there will normally come a point at which one or both parties instinctively feels that it's time to move things on a little. There are no hard and fast rules with this – 'Just do small talk for 7 minutes and then you must talk business' – so you need to be aware of signals that may mean it is appropriate to conversationally 'move on'. Peter Collett's *The Book of Tells* is a great place to learn more about conversational cues.

Here are some to start you off:

- 'So, Jane, what brings you to this event this afternoon?'
- 'I see from your delegate badge that you work for Nexen. What do they do?'
- 'Oh, you normally get off at Bank. Is your office far from there? What exactly is it that you do?'
- 'Real Estate team – what does that mean you do at BLP?'

All the above are what I might term 'linking' questions, great for moving on to work-related stuff. Asking questions is good, because as every sales person knows, selling is not about being able to talk, it's about asking questions, shutting up and listening.

There are two reasons for this:

- It's interesting to learn more about what other people do.
- The more you learn about someone's business, the easier it is to discover whether what you sell might be of value to them. If it is, and you get on with them, then that's what's going to prompt you to get a business card from them and follow up! If that's not the case, then at least you will have increased your knowledge of business generally, have shared a good old chat with them, but probably not felt the need to ask for a business card, put them on your database or invite them to one of your riveting seminars.

Just as there are topics of social small talk, there are topics of business small talk too.

This could be general, such as the country's finances or the economic outlook. Then each sector has its topics of small talk: local government, construction, defence, law, accountancy, retail and so on.

Each sector then has areas within that, so taking law as an example these include construction, employment, real estate, plus many more. Sure enough, each one of those has certain subjects and issues that form the topics of conversation.

So if you are targeting the commercial property sector, for instance, then you should know what's going on in that field (no pun intended). You won't know as much as the surveyors or agents or lawyers you're talking to, but a read through the latest copy of the relevant trade press (probably *Estates Gazette*) will give you a sufficient overview to be able to contribute to conversations and ask intelligent questions. That all adds to your credibility.

Listening

Talking is all well and good, but it's listening that really holds the key in developing relationships.

We live in an age where we are bombarded by people and organizations attempting to get our attention. As a result, we are in what might be best described as a state of 'continual partial attention'. We hear everything but listen to nothing. It's like sitting in front of a conveyor belt of information: we see it but we register very little. The *Metro* newspaper sums up what I mean very neatly: we pick it up, read it and leave it, having got the merest taste of what's going on in the world but not knowing about anything in any depth or detail. In short, we graze.

However, when you want to get to know someone, when you are looking out for the next client, when you want to *CONNECT* with them, then you have to listen to them, really listen. Not hear, listen.

You hear with your ears but you listen with your eyes. We all know this, which is why, when a man is watching the telly and a woman starts speaking to him, she knows that she is wasting her time, because even though he may say he's listening, he's not. He can hear her, but he sure as hell isn't listening.

Really listening means listening and deriving meaning from what's said. Often, particularly in networking situations, we get so fixated on what we think we should be telling the prospect about our service or product that we are not listening to what the other person is saying, we're preparing our answer.

If you want to know more about the body language that lets you know when someone is listening to you, buy yourself a copy of Collett's *The Book of Tells* or Barbara and Allan Pease's *The Definitive Guide to Body Language*.

The only thing I'm going to mention here is that whether your stance or what you are doing with your body is comfortable for you is not of paramount importance. When you are talking to another person it's not about how you feel, it's about how *they* feel – and that should not be intimidated, uncomfortable or pressured. You could be the most fascinating person on the planet, but if you're standing too close to or you keep touching the person you're talking to, they're going to leave as quickly as possible, with a bad impression. And even if what you had to sell was of tremendous value to them, they wouldn't ever buy from you. They'd rather go elsewhere, even if it meant paying more for a slightly inferior product.

How to Move On

Many people ask me how to get away from dull people. Although I'd be the first to admit that there are quite a few members of the 'seriously dull club', they don't tend to be in business or go to networking events. And while, as I've said, not everyone you meet will end up being a client, it's quite rare to meet someone who's not interesting. Maybe not straight away, on first meeting, but once you get talking, the vast majority of us do have something interesting to talk about regarding the experiences and adventures we've had.

Anyway, you've been chatting to someone for a while and you feel that the conversation has run its course. You may want to get an opportunity to meet this person again and chat further about matters that have arisen or areas that you have in common business-wise, but for now you want to move on to someone else.

First of all, *do not* fall back on 'If you'll excuse me I need to go and freshen up my drink' or 'If you'll excuse me I need to pop to the loo'. The problem with both of these is that the other person may decide that they need to do the same and end up following you. While someone accompanying you to the drinks area might be a bit of a pain when you wanted to get away from them, it's not half as awkward as them either sitting in the cubicle or standing next to you while you're both having a wee.

I'm going to furnish you with two options here, both of which work well and both of which require you to be assertive – and one that represents the very zenith of networking ability.

Tip One: Be Honest

I'll illustrate the first tip with some dialogue:

> *'Well, Tim, it's been lovely to chat to you this evening and hear about your business and the stuff that's going on, but there are a few other people I'd like to catch up with while I'm here, so if you'll excuse me I'll go and seek them out.'*

This is assertive, honest and unambiguous.

Some people feel it's a little bit mean, because it does result in leaving the other person to fend for themselves. But Tim's a grown up. He's been to networking events before and he understands that you aren't there to spend the next two hours with him. If he's the sort of guy who can't handle parting, then maybe he should ring the Samaritans.

Tip Two: Introduce Them to Someone Else

When I think of networking being done well, one person always comes to mind: Vincent Connor. I've known Vincent since 2000, when I met him in my capacity as director of a recruitment business and he was heading up the Glasgow office of the law firm formerly known as Masons (now Pinsent Masons). Vincent moved on to head up the firm's activities right across Scotland and Northern Ireland, before leaving to sunnier, slightly more humid climes to run the Far East Asian region of the firm. He now sits in a big office block in Hong Kong and is no doubt wooing the locals with his urbane Scottish charm.

What Vincent has in common with all good networkers is his ability to move around a room like a social butterfly. To watch him do this was superb. He'd welcome people with a warm, genuine smile, move easily into small talk and then glide effortlessly on to business matters.

One of his fortes, however, was moving on. Rather than leave someone on their own, he'd ask them if they knew 'Joanne' or 'Dave' or one of any number of people with whom he was acquainted. Again, I'll use dialogue to illustrate my point:

> **VINCENT:** *Nick, have you had the pleasure of meeting Joanne from KPMG yet?*
> **ME:** *No, I can't say I have.*
> **VINCENT:** *Oh well, let me introduce you to her. She's just over there.*

He'd then guide me across to where Joanne was standing talking to some other people, but while doing so would give me a bit of background on her, like where she used to work, whether she had kids, where she went to university or what hobby or sport she was into. Then the conversation would go like this:

> **Vincent:** *Hi Jo, sorry to interrupt, but there's someone I'd really like you to meet. Nick, Joanne. Joanne, Nick Davies from the Scottish Legal Awards. Nick's originally from Manchester/is a big footie fan/does a bit of stand-up comedy/used to run a catering business.*

He'd choose something where he knew there was a connection or link between the two of us. Once the introduction was complete, he'd make his farewells, excuse himself and move on to someone else or a group of people.

You may be thinking that you'd have to know a bit about a few people for this to work, and I wouldn't deny that. However, there are a great number of occasions when you do know at least one person at an event – and one will do.

Introducing someone to another contact is moving from 'networking' to 'connecting' people and is lovely for everyone concerned.

It's good for you because you can move on to the next person in the knowledge that you haven't left your current contact having to find someone else.

It works for your contact because they're not in the awkward position of having to chat to a stranger and don't feel abandoned.

It works for the person to whom you have introduced your contact, because they have now met someone new without having to go and talk to a stranger or break in to a group.

And here's another thing. My contact and I might have had a good natter, swapped a bit of small talk, got on well enough, but there has been no business connection. Just because this encounter is not going to lead to anything, it doesn't necessarily follow that the same will be the case for them and another person. They could get on like a house on fire and end up having a very profitable business relationship.

Think of this as like the dating game. In the course of trying to find the ideal partner, you will meet a lot of people you like, get on with and have a laugh with; it doesn't necessarily mean that you want to take it further or that just because they aren't the 'right one' for you, they aren't absolutely right for someone else. Once again, the message surrounding networking has to be *relax* – it's about chatting to people. If business springs from it, great; if it doesn't, it's not the end of the world.

Following Up

So relax, indulge in appropriate small talk, listen and be aware of how you are making the person to whom you are speaking feel. Be polite but assertive. Connect and introduce people to one another, write stuff down and always look the part.

Networking – at the right events – allows you to get through the *CONNECT* and *MEET* stages of the model simultaneously.

If you've read this book from the beginning, as opposed to skipping to the bits that take your fancy, and I've done my job properly, you should have *FOLLOW UP* and keeping control at every stage imprinted in your brain.

However, I now want to examine in detail how you follow up after meeting someone at a networking event. Having trained and coached many thousands of people in all manner of organizations, this is the single biggest area of concern for the vast majority of them – so it's to this that the next chapter turns.

FOLLOWING UP

MAKING THE MOST OF THE CONTACTS YOU MAKE – EFFICIENTLY, EFFECTIVELY AND ELEGANTLY

L et me reiterate: following up is something that you should do *at every stage of the business development process*. At each and every stage you must let people know what you are going to do next and when you are going to do it – *every single time*!

Following Up after a Networking Event

Networking is great, but it's about as useful as a long-term commitment with Jordan if you aren't going to follow up.

Depending on which books or websites you read, you'll soon discover that it takes between five and seven contacts with a potential customer before they become an actual customer. What is more, the same all-knowing business-type gurus also assert that few people bother to follow up, even once, after the initial encounter.

This is daft, because if you've gone to the effort of getting yourself on a delegate list, smartened yourself up, pitched up at the networking event, secured the name badge to your chest, taken your courage in hand and gone and talked to some people, it seems like a dreadful waste if all you do by way of maintaining contact is sending an 'it was lovely to meet you' email with a pdf of something utterly enthralling attached and the killer final line: 'If there's anything else I can help you with, please don't hesitate to call.'

Don't get me wrong, I only follow up with people who meet two criteria:

- I like them; and
- I think that what I offer would be good for them.

I'm not going to try to arrange to see them in order to 'sell' to them in the traditional sense. I genuinely want to find out more about them, their role and organization and then, only if I think there is something I do that they'd like and would be of benefit to them, will I tell them about it.

So, let's assume you've met someone, you get on and you reckon that what you do or what you've got would be of use to them. But somehow you've met a good number of people like this and all you have to show for it is a big pile of business cards on your desk or arranged alphabetically in that neat business-card holder you got from the stationery cupboard. You're not sure whether to write to them, phone or email, so what you in fact do is put them on a mailing list and invite them to a seminar. You figure that if, over a period of months or even years, you send enough invitations, they will one day attend and end up buying your product or using your service.

That's convoluted, tortuous and terribly long-winded and, in common with not targeting your networking, is a massive waste of time and effort.

I have a process for following up that I've honed and perfected over the past 23 years – and it works. Sure, amend it, make it personal to you, but don't deviate too far from it. I built a successful sandwich business, legal recruitment business, an awards programme and more recently a training consultancy from a standing start on this exact process.

It hasn't got a fancy name, nor is there an instantly forgettable acronym to run alongside it. It works if you want to break into a new market, a new sector or a new geographical area (I only know that it works in the UK and Ireland. It might do the business in Europe, the Middle or Far East or North America, but since I haven't tried it, I don't know.) It works if you are starting from scratch or developing a bigger market share in an area that's familiar to you already.

Step One: Follow Up While Still at the Event

The really important point, the bit you cannot miss out, is that you should line up a follow-up meeting right there and then, rather than waiting a few days and then trying to do it. For example:

> **YOU:** *Sally, it's been great to meet you and have a chat. I've been really interested in what you had to say about your firm/your business/your plans for the future. There are a couple of other people I'd really like to meet here today, but it'd be great to continue our conversation/ chat and find out more about what you do over a coffee some time. Would that be OK?*

This is not a definitive 'script'. I don't want to you to learn this and quote it verbatim. You will find your own form of words, but make sure you keep it relaxed and light (kind of 'semi-skimmed selling'). You will notice that I don't talk about having a 'meeting' and that I refer to 'coffee'. 'Coffee' conjures up Starbucks, Caffe Nero, Costa – informal, neutral, no pressure, which is exactly what it should be.

Relationships (all relationships) are like fires: you have to keep them going otherwise they grow cold, dark and sad. You've established a relationship when you met and talked to this person, so the fire, no matter how small, is kindled; you don't want it to go out, but it will even if you leave it for just a few days.

Remember those hot plates I banged on about in the chapter about targeting? Well, the analogy applies equally at this stage of the business development process.

When you are talking face to face with someone, the relationship is *HOT*. As soon as you part company it begins to cool, which means that if you wait a few days before getting in touch, it's going to be harder to secure their commitment and is made even more difficult because you are doing it over the phone or via email, rather than in person.

So, having suggested you could meet up sometime over a coffee, what do you think their reply will be?

SALLY: *Yeah, sure, that'd be nice.*

I have *never* had someone say 'No' and neither will you. British people will not look you in the eye at this point and decline your offer; it's just too rude.

If they don't want to meet up then they will let you know, but not right there and then; they'll do that later and by email – which is fine (but more of that later on).

So let's assume that Sally agrees.

YOU: *Great, I'll give you a ring before the end of the week/beginning of the next and we'll put a date in the diary.*

If the time frame you've stated is not good for her – 'Oh, not next week, because I'm on holiday' – then tell her that you'll get in touch the following week.

There's also another closing technique hidden in there. Did you spot it?

Read the paragraph again.

It's something we've already met, called the 'assumptive close'.

I haven't asked 'When shall I ring you to set something up?' or said 'to see if you would be free to meet up for a coffee'. What I have said – quite deliberately – is: 'I'll give you a ring before the end of the week/beginning of next' followed by 'and we'll put a date in the diary'. I have just assumed that this meeting is going to go ahead; there's no doubt about it in my mind.

You then part company and either later on at the event, on your way home or in the office the next day, you note down the salient points of information you picked up during the small talk, in particular anything that she is doing or is involved with prior to when you've said you will get in touch. You do this so that when you do, you have something to say by way of an introduction: 'How did your trip to Swansea go?' or 'I remember you mentioned you were going to a wedding last weekend, how did it go?'

Not only is this kind of question a relaxed and non-pressured way to get the conversation going, it lets the other person know that you were listening to them. Believe me, that fact alone will put you in the top 10% of people they've ever met at a networking event! It builds rapport and that's what good sales people do.

Step Two: The 'Holding' Email

If I've met Sally and done the 'It would be great to meet up some time over a coffee' routine, to which she has agreed, and then I say I'll ring before the end of the week, on my return to the office I sometimes whizz off a holding email, which goes along these lines:

> *Hi Sally, Nick here – the tall Mancunian bloke with a thing for shoes – just a quick note to say how nice it was to meet you yesterday/earlier on and to let you know that I'll be in touch before the end of the week to fix a date up for that coffee.*

Again, you'll note that the tone is relaxed and informal and that I am giving her a quick prompt as to who I am.

Step Two is also important because it highlights two things that you must always do when promoting your services, both of which I've already mentioned:

- Tell them what you are going to do next.
- Tell them when you are going to do it.

People in business loathe surprises. They like nice, steady, predictable growth. Surprises mean having to draw up a new plan or attend interminable strategy meetings. So let the prospect know at every single step of the process what it is you are going to do and when you're going to do it.

Step Three: Using the Phone
Do what you said you'd do, when you said you'd do it.

So, if you said you'd drop her an email before the end of the week, then guess what? Ditto if you said you'd give her a ring. If you just said you'd be in touch then either option's open to you, although I prefer the phone.

Why phone?
Back in 1971 a bright young chap by the name of Albert Merhabian (now Emeritus Professor of Psychology at UCLA) sat in a lab in his white coat and, following extensive research, arrived at the conclusion that if, when someone speaks, they lack confidence or belief in what they are saying, the listener will unconsciously analyse the speaker's communication according to the following percentages: 7% weight to the words he hears; 38% to the pitch, tone, pace and volume of his voice; but a whopping 55% to the speaker's body language.

In other words if the words he speaks don't 'match' what his body 'says', then the listener will always believe the latter, because it's very difficult to fake. Anyone can say that they 'love you', but you know if they mean it by the way they say it and how they behave.

So I use the phone, because I'm getting 45% impact rather than only the 7% available to me via email. What is more – and here's where you want to be a little assertive – it's harder for someone to say 'No' to you over the phone, if they've changed their mind. This is a little, tiny bit of pressure, but that's OK.

The phone call

Bear in mind what I said regarding the timing of cold calls. Never ring on a Monday. Call at the less busy times between about 10.30 and 11.30 am or 2.30 and 4.30 pm.

If you get through, here's what you say:

> **YOU:** *Hi Sally, it's Nick here, you recall we met the other evening at the X event. I'm the guy that used to be a lawyer and has a thing about shoes.*

You need to refresh her memory, since she might well have met any number of people since you. There's nothing worse than someone calling you and they start going on about something, while all the while you're trying to work out who they are, let alone when you met them.

Once she's placed you, now's a good time either to indulge in a little small talk and refer back to things that you made a note of on her business card, or to get straight to the point.

Again, there are no hard-and-fast rules about this: you sense that some people are up for a chat and others aren't; it depends what mood they're in. At first you aren't going to get this right every time, but don't beat yourself up about it: the more you do it the better you'll get.

Once any small talk is done or if small talk seems inappropriate, you need to tell her why you are calling:

> **YOU:** *Anyway, I'm calling to arrange a time for that coffee we talked about and wondered whether later this week or next week was better?*

You're being up front and getting straight to the point. You're not using aggressive language or tone, but you do know what you want. She did know you were going to get in touch to arrange something (no surprises, remember). I'm also using the alternative close, as I discussed in chapter 4.

If you get voicemail

If you get through to your contact's voicemail, you have to leave a message.

I've already talked about trust and credibility (see chapter 3) being the essential ingredients for effective persuasion. So if you have told her that you will call before the end of the week, then you must demonstrate that you've done just that. If you don't, it sows a tiny seed of doubt in their mind as to whether you are a person of your word.

The message needs to include the following:

- Your name
- Where you met
- Why you are calling – to set up a time to meet
- What you are going to do next
- Your number

It could go something like this:

> **YOU:** *Hi Susan, it's Nick here. You recall we met last Thursday at the Lawyers in the City do; I was the tall Mancunian bloke who commented on your great shoes. Anyway, I'm ringing so that we can put a date in the diary to meet up and have a natter, as I said I would. I'll*

*try you again later this week, but in the meantime if you
get a minute then you can always give me a call. My
number is 0777 777 777. Thanks.*

This is a bit like the holding email in that it's relaxed, informal but
also assumes that we will meet up. However, it adds my number
because if she rings me back, then bingo!

If you leave a message and a potential client calls you, that's what
sales people refer to as a 'buying sign'. It's very rare that someone will
call you back to say they have changed their mind – they'll normally
prefer email for that, so if you do get a call it usually means they are
interested. 'Interested' in meeting up, that is. They might have an
inkling that you might well be able to provide them with something
they need, but the only thing you want them to be interested in at
this point is meeting up with you.

This is a very important point. *You're not selling your wares over the
telephone or via email.* The *only* thing you are 'selling' here is a chat
over a coffee. The only thing you want from her is her time.

She knows that you are not meeting up for a social. She also knows
that ultimately you would like her to buy stuff from you. She's not
stupid, but thus far you've made it all so relaxed and pleasant that
she's happy to meet up.

I've already said that people buy from people they like and that selling
is about making it easy for people to buy. If arranging to meet up
with you is easy and pleasant, then the chances are that working with
you will be just the same. What you are doing right from the first
meeting – formal or informal – is letting the person know that you
would be easy to work with.

Step Four: If She Doesn't Reply

Leave it a week or perhaps a little bit longer before you try again. I
reckon that somewhere between a week and two weeks is best.

If she picks up the phone then you're up and running. If not, leave a voicemail similar to the first one, but add that you're still keen to meet up.

Step Five: If You Still Haven't Heard Back

If another couple of weeks goes by and still you've heard nothing, send an email.

The email should be similar to the voicemail you've left: informal, relaxed, chatty and containing the same info – tell her why you're emailing and tell her what you're going to do next.

The only thing I add in the email is a bit about the fact that I've already tried to get hold of the person via phone. A typical email from me would go like this:

> *Hi Susan*
>
> *I've left a couple of voicemails over the past few weeks but with no luck, so I thought I'd send you an email, since I know that sometimes it's a lot less hassle to reply then setting aside time to make a call.*
>
> *I'm still dead keen to meet up and have a chat and am in your area on the 6th and 7th of July, so hopefully we can put a date in the diary.*
>
> *In the meantime I've put some stuff about what I do in the post just so you can get a better feel for it.*
>
> *Nick*

Once again, it's relaxed and I'm using a laid-back alternative close by suggesting some dates. If she comes back to me and says she cannot do those dates, then I know she's looked in her diary, which tells me she's interested.

I'm also telling her what I'm going to do next – send her some stuff about what I do. Notice that I haven't used the word 'literature'. Literature is what Jane Austen, Dickens and Thackeray produced; I don't. Sometimes I'll favour the term 'info' or 'information' instead.

In a minute I'll look in detail at the covering letter I send with that 'info', but at this stage it's important to appreciate the importance of email. The really great thing about email at this point in the process is that it allows the person I want to meet to say 'No'. And I want it to be easy for her to say 'No'.

I said right at the start of this section that no one in the UK would turn round and say no to you if you suggested, at the end of your initial chat with them at the networking event, that you meet up for a coffee next time you were in their area. You may also recall that if they weren't interested, they'd tell you later. Well, this is when they'll do it.

If someone you are talking to agrees – albeit informally – to meeting up for a chat at some point in the future, it is terribly difficult for them then to turn you down when you ring and speak to them. Human beings like to be consistent and agreeing to something then changing their mind is a really awkward thing to do.

However, if we do change our mind it's so much easier to tell the other person via email because it distances us from the message. Of course, the response to your email will not be 'Sorry, Nick, but I've changed my mind and I don't want to meet for a chat over a coffee', it'll be delivered with a little excuse:

Hi Nick
Sorry I've not been back to you earlier but things are a bit hectic here, what with graduate recruitment and trainee induction.

I wonder if we might put meeting up on hold for the time being until I can get some breathing space in my diary.
Sally

This is OK. Don't take it personally, don't get upset and don't get defensive or pushy. They are obviously too busy and quite frankly you don't want to be wasting time – theirs or yours – sitting drinking coffee, if they don't want to really be there.

But don't give up. You must acknowledge the message with something like this:

No worries at all, Sally, I completely understand.
When's best for me to get back in touch: October or perhaps the start of next year? (Make these dates roughly three and six months apart.)
In the meantime you've got all my info, so if anything comes up that I can help you with then give me a shout.
Nick

Relaxed and informal. It's no big deal that she doesn't want to see me *yet*. She isn't saying 'never', just not yet. I'm using the alternative close again: telling her what I'm going to do and offering her an alternative for when I'm going to do it.

It's my experience that in the vast majority of cases, the person will come back to me having selected one or two of the options, in which case I'll make a note in my diary and confirm that I'll be in touch when she suggests. You are always 'leaving the door open' to get back in touch. Never shut things off completely, because you never know what's going to happen and neither does the other person. Circumstances change, so always *FOLLOW UP*.

Sending a letter

Sending a letter is one of the steps in the follow-up process, but I don't have a hard-and-fast rule about when to do so. I might send one following the first or second voicemail and occasionally after the first email.

Earlier on I ran through an example of a typical letter I might send in chapter 4, but I'll furnish you with another here:

Hello James

I've called a couple of times to try to speak to you but with no luck, so yesterday – the 29th – I left a voicemail to let you know that I'd be sending you some information about what I do – here it is.

I'm a former lawyer and have worked with many thousands of lawyers, which means I understand how frustrating it can sometimes be trying to persuade a bunch of highly intelligent solicitors just how vital it is that they are relaxed and chatty at networking events and, equally, that a 45-slide PowerPoint presentation just isn't going to woo a potential client in a pitch for business. What I deliver is practical, down-to-earth training that people enjoy and learn from; all delivered without the use of PowerPoint.

Although I've delivered training to all the major law firms in the City, I've yet to do things for firms in the North West, which is a crying shame since I'm a Mancunian now living in Edinburgh but always keen to 'go home'. I also know that there are some cracking partnerships there as well.

I have appointments to meet the HR/training managers of about eight firms in the region over the next couple of months and would really like to pop in and chat to you, find out how you go about training and whether what I do might help.

I'll give you a call in the next few days and hopefully we can put something in the diary.

Regards

Nick

I want you to understand what I'm doing here, so let's take this letter apart, a paragraph at a time:

- An informal start – I've met this guy so why would I begin it any other way?
- Just letting him know I've been in touch.
- A bit of humour, which also lets him know that I know what being in his shoes is like.
- I'm busy with big organizations, but I'd like to do more with other firms, plus a bit of relaxed humour (I'm a regular guy).
- People like you in firms like yours in your neck of the woods have agreed to see me – credibility, 'don't miss out' and I'm probably worth 30 minutes of your time.
- Keeping control – letting him know what I'm going to do next and when.

Step Six: If You *Still* Haven't Heard a Thing (The Pain in the Backside Email)

You've left two messages on their voicemail, you've sent an email and written a letter with some of your company info along with it, but alas, still no response. What should you do? Give up? Call it a day? Get nasty or make it personal? Find out where their kids go to school and follow them?

You've got to face facts, they're either really busy or they really don't want to see you. Either way, you must find out.

In this kind of case I send an email like the following.

Sent: 12 June 09:32
To: Kevin
Subject: A bit of a pain

Morning Kevin

I'm still keen to meet up and have a chat. However, following a couple of voicemails, a letter and an email, I'm acutely aware of rapidly becoming a pain in the backside.

So, I'll not be bothering you again until the start of next year, when I'll get in touch just to see where you're up to and whether my timing is better.

Regards

Nick

Note the time of my email and that of his response:

Date: 12 Jun 09:55

To: Nick

Subject: RE: A bit of a pain

Hi Nick,

Not at all.

Apologies for not coming back to you, things are rather hectic at the moment. I received your literature and as yet have not read it. Perhaps you could give me a call in a month and we can take it from there.

Regards

Kevin

I rarely have to send this kind of email and I do, on occasion, tone it down and use 'pain in the neck' instead of 'backside'. However, the recipient gets the point. I won't get in touch again until some time way in the future. However, you will note that even in this 'final' correspondence I am still letting them know what I'm going to do and when I intend doing it.

Roughly half of the people I send this to reply and the majority of them apologize profusely for having not got back to me sooner. Some then go on to suggest a date, while others acknowledge that they are very busy and that they appreciate the fact that I've recognized that.

As for those who don't have the decency to respond in any way? Well, then I get to say one of my favourite words in sales:

'NEXT!'

Irrespective of what you manufacture or what service you provide, you should never, ever beg for business. Even if winning this client would be the deal of the century. Even if you've lain awake at night imagining being able to tell people that you got the X account. Don't ever seem desperate for their business.

Keen yes. Focused yes. Determined most definitely, but never desperate. Needy people are very unattractive.

There comes a time when you have to – and I'm going to use the oven analogy again – 'put it on the back burner'.

There are plenty of potential clients I have contacted and seen. There have even been those who have expressed a most definite intention to buy what I'm offering, but then failed to communicate. In these situations – if I'm alone in my office – I shout 'NEXT!'

Even if your job is solely devoted to bringing in business, you must recognize when it's time to move on. If developing business is something that you have to make time for in your job (and since this book is aimed at you, I suspect that's the case), then you really haven't got time to mess about with people who haven't got the common decency to simply say 'Thanks but no thanks'. And they're probably not the type of people you want to be doing business with anyway.

I've said all along that selling is about making it easy for people to buy, but have you ever noticed that your favourite clients are the ones who make it easy for you to deliver?

My best clients – the ones I love doing work with, whether that's a lot or just a little – are the ones who are polite, get back to me, let me know what's going on, are up front, who want a good rate for the job but don't expect something for nothing and don't try to screw every penny of discount from me. These are the people I am happy to do extra bits and pieces for without upping my fee or on occasion not charging them at all, because they are relationships built on mutual respect and trust.

Have you ever noticed that it's those potential clients who were a pain to get hold of, who messed you about, cancelled things, let you down, bargained you down for a big discount with the promise of 'loads more where that came from', who turned out to be even more trouble when you finally got to supply them with something?

Read the signs, ladies and gents: if they're getting on your nerves now, you can bet they'll be doing it in the future. Ditch them now!

NEXT!

Following Up on Follow Up

That's a pretty detailed look at *FOLLOW UP* but it's simple. While I'd be the first to concede that there are probably other ways to do it, all I can tell you is that I've built a very nice little business from scratch following these steps – with everyone on my target list and those I've met at events.

As with other stuff in this book, try it and see how you get on. Take what works and cut, paste, delete, alter or amend what doesn't.

CHAPTER 8

MEET

MAKING THE MOST OF THE ENCOUNTER AND ENSURING YOU KEEP IN CONTROL

Whether you have connected successfully with someone via a cold call or at a networking event, you'll have arrived at a point where you are about to *MEET* – the third stage in our business development process.

Sure, we've invented tonnes of novel ways to communicate with one another: email, phone, videoconference, teleconference, Skype, Facebook and so on. All have their merits, but I don't care what anyone says: if you really want to know whether you should spend decent money with someone on something that matters to you, you feel much better if you've met them properly.

The 'sit down, let's have a chat about our businesses' is where we find out whether we want to buy from this person: do we trust them and their product? The meeting is about the face-to-face stuff. It's about putting the prospect at ease with some small talk. It's about creating an atmosphere that's professional yet relaxed. It's about asking the right questions, shutting up, noting down what you learn. It's also about keeping control and not leaving – under any circumstances — without them knowing that you are keen on working with them. And it's always about you parting with both of you knowing what's going to happen next and when it's going to happen.

The Meeting

The purpose of this meeting is to find out about the person, their role, more about the business, and whether what you have on offer might be of interest to them.

Some people get bogged down in listing lots and lots of questions in such meetings. I don't: for me, this is more about seeing whether we get on but with a bit of information gathering on the side.

Choosing the Venue

Unless circumstances dictate otherwise, I would always plump for going to visit the other person. It shows that you are keen and prepared to go out of your way, you learn loads more and because they are 'at home', they're relaxed, which means more open and more forthcoming. It also opens up the possibility of meeting other relevant people within their organization while you're there.

I recently went to a firm in Bristol to meet the HR and training manager, with whom I was getting on really well, when she mentioned that although she wished to go ahead and use me to do some training, it was her boss, David, who had the final say. So naturally, I asked if it would be possible just to say hello to him, if he was in the office. As it happens he was but couldn't see me. However, it's always worth asking.

If going to their place is not an option, then a coffee shop convenient to them is my venue of choice. I always pay and so should you, or at least offer to pay. It's polite and brings in that bit of reciprocity I mentioned earlier. Always opt for coffee rather than lunch. Lunch is too formal, difficult to make notes during, commits them to at least an hour and a half and is just too intimate at the beginning of a relationship.

Taking Other People Along

There might be occasions where you think the person you are meeting would benefit from seeing one of your colleagues at the same time. I wouldn't rule this out, but you must always ask them if they mind, during the correspondence between you when setting the meeting up. To turn up without having run it passed them could be viewed as a tad pushy. You must explain to the person you are meeting why you think it would be of benefit to them to meet this second guest.

A partner at a law firm I recently worked with told a story of having come from an in-house role, inviting a former colleague to meet for lunch, just to make sure the relationship was still strong and to see if there was a possibility of him being given work from his previous firm, only to have two partners get wind of it and invite themselves along for the meal. While I'm sure their intentions were good, their new colleague felt awkward at turning up 'mob-handed'; but not half as uncomfortable as his former colleague, who felt as though he had been ambushed and was being press-ganged into pushing business their way. Three onto one is not fair!

Before You Set Off

This is obvious, but I make no apology for bringing it to your attention. Make sure that you know where you're going. If the organization has more than one office, check to see which one the person is expecting to meet you at.

Print off a map, get the relevant A to Z, boot up the satnav and be sure of your route and how you are going to get there – bus, cab, tube, plane or whatever. And make sure you know how long it will take and then add some time to allow for delays, hold-ups and missed trains.

Six months ago I needed to get to Uxbridge. I knew that the Piccadilly line ended there, but didn't appreciate that it takes nearly an hour from Holborn. Because it was on the tube network, in common with many people not native to London I had just assumed that no journey was ever going to be more than about 20 minutes' duration. Needless to say, once I realized I was going to be late I immediately got in touch with the person I was meeting, explained the position and apologized profusely.

It's my experience that most people are quite understanding and accommodating when visitors are late, but only so long as you let them know and apologize. It's not knowing that annoys the pants off people.

Professional sales people are rarely late, because they understand the important role that trust and dependability play in securing business. In fact, let me tell you a story that illustrates my point and tells you something about how sales people regard training as well.

A few years back I delivered a one-day course on presentation skills to three senior sales managers. It was held in a small conference room at a hotel adjacent to Heathrow airport. The course began at 9.30 am. One of the delegates had flown in from Houston, Texas, the other from Rio de Janeiro and another from Dubai. With the exception of the guy from Texas – who had got the wrong airport, landed at Gatwick but telephoned me, apologized and explained that he'd be 15 minutes late (in the event he was 12) – they turned up on time, participated in the course and then flew back to their respective home cities.

The feedback? Thankfully they all loved the course, but thought that it should be a week long.

The moral of the story is that sales people hate being late and even if they have to fly halfway across the world to learn something new, they will do, if they think that it will give them the edge over their competitors. Stephen Covey, in his renowned book *The 7 Habits of Highly Effective People*, lists habit number 7 as

'Sharpen the Saw'. In other words, keep learning and giving yourself the edge.

Indeed, as I type I am listening to Sir Clive Woodward being interviewed on *Desert Island Discs* and he has just told Kirsty Young that in his office hangs a sign that reads:

'Better Never Stops'

Another thing you should get into the habit of doing is ensuring that you have a pen, paper, diary, business card and any other information about your firm that you need to take. You may have seen an article in a newspaper written by an employee or perhaps one featuring the company as a whole. In either case, take it with you or simply make a note of the salient points. These sorts of things can be little belters in terms of moving the conversation on from small talk to business talk.

Email to Confirm

A day or two prior to the meeting, send an email just to check that all's well to go ahead as arranged.

Once again, bitter experience has taught me the importance of this. I once set off at 5 am to drive from Manchester for a 9.30 am meeting in Norwich, at which it had already been agreed that a contract was going to be signed that meant a decent amount of commission for me. I got there only to have the other person sit me down in his office and tell me that he'd changed his mind.

I'm not proud to say that it was the one and only time I slammed a door when leaving a customer's office. However, on my drive back from Norwich and having calmed down a little, I realized that a quick phone call (this was the days before email) the day before would have saved me a wasted trip and him what I'm sure must have been a cracked pane of glass in his door.

Do Your Research

A lot of people seem to think this is a major exercise, involving meticulous research and in-depth analysis of articles, clippings and all manner of data. It's not.

Take a look at the organization's website to get a feel for it, find out what it does, where its offices are and, while you're at it, put all that info into your CRM system – if you work for a firm that's got one – or just in the notebook, database or other record-keeping system that you use. Make a few notes and then when you're in the meeting you can ask a few questions based around what you've learned.

When, during the meeting, the contact asks me how much I know about their firm, I usually mention a few things, but then say something along the lines of:

> *To be honest, I don't know that much, which is why I prefer to come out and see people; I find that I get a much better feel of what an organization is about when I pay a visit than anything I can learn from a website.*

On the Day

As you've probably sussed by now – and again, it's obvious – get to their offices early. Ten minutes before the meeting is good, although turning up at reception 15 minutes early is a bit too much. On the rare occasions that happens to me – it's pouring with rain and the cab has dropped me right at the door – then I let the receptionist know that I'm early and not to ring my contact yet. I don't want them to feel under pressure to hurry and finish whatever they are doing.

You know what it's like. If you've arranged for someone to come to your house at 10 am and they turn up at 9.50, it can really throw you. With 10 minutes to go you're just readying yourself for their arrival – maybe a quick pop to the loo or application of lipstick, or just enough time to hang the washing out or set the table. Well, it's no different for people at work. They may have given themselves 10 minutes prior to the meeting in which to take a look at your website or re-read the letter you sent them, or glance through your brochure and jot down a few questions they want to ask you.

If you are able to see someone perhaps up to an hour prior to the agreed time, it's worth dropping them an email to ask if bringing the meeting forward would suit them better. Occasionally it does and then they're really pleased. Make sure when you do get in touch that you make it quite clear that you are very happy to stick with the agreed time and that you are simply giving them option of the earlier time because it might be helpful and more convenient for them.

In Reception

OK, you have gone into reception and let the person behind the desk know that you've arrived. The chances are that the first thing they will ask you to do is sign the visitor's book.

This little, much overlooked book is a fount of useful information, so when you sign in, make sure that you take your time to complete each section neatly and slowly, because as you write in your details you should be scanning the page to see who else has visited the company and, more importantly, the person you're going to be meeting. In particular, you're looking to see if any of your competitors have been in. What you learn here is not going to form the basis of any conversation you have with your potential client, but it's good background information to have in mind.

Once the book is signed and you have in your possession the security pass, you should ask the receptionist where the loo is, even if you don't need to go. Wash your hands, check your hair, your teeth, your nose, that buttons, zips and ties are done up and that your shoes are clean.

Once back in reception, try to avoid sitting down. Modern reception furniture tends to consist of huge, comfy sofas in black leather. The sort you can sink right into, settle back, grab a paper from the glass coffee table and get comfy with. Except there's a downside: it's devilishly hard to extricate yourself!

So in walks the guy you are due to meet and as he stands over you and proffers his hand in order for you to shake it, you are left attempting to slide yourself forward sufficiently to get some decent leverage with your feet on the ground, while at the same time pushing down with your arms into the deeply pliant, slightly shiny leather so you can push your body up, all the while conscious that his hand is still outstretched awaiting yours. When you do finally get yourself into an upright position, your hand is now black with newsprint and slightly damp because of the length of time it's been in contact with the leather. Nice start!

So stand in reception. You want to greet the person you are meeting on the same level.

Do read the file that contains press clippings (loads of firms have them out on the table). Do also look at any awards on display, as these will provide opening topics of conversation.

If you are asked to wait in the meeting room for the person you are seeing, do not sit down. Wait until they come in and indicate where they are going to sit before you plump for your seat. If it's a rectangular or square table, the best position is at right angles to your prospect (see the diagram).

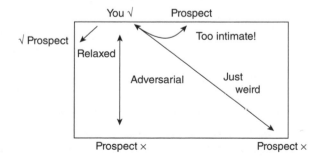

Accept a drink. Even if it's water and you just sip it, it's polite and creates a more relaxed environment.

I visit loads of offices that occupy floors many storeys high and more often than not that makes for a decent view. If so, comment on it to your host when they enter the room. It's a relaxed opener and you'll be amazed how many people join you at the window and start giving a bird's-eye-view tour of the vista in front of you.

In the Meeting

You've both settled in. Drinks have been poured, biscuits selected and now it's time to kick things off with a bit of small talk. If you've done the 'what a delightful view' bit, then the other small-talk standards are fine.

That said, if there are photos of their children on the wall or paintings done by their kids, then comment on those. People who don't have children will be aware just how much those of us with them like to talk about them. And people with children are well aware of just what a rich seam of small talk kids can provide.

Eventually, however, the small talk has to cease and the business at hand must be addressed. I think that when such a point arrives, you should be up front. I often say something along the lines of: 'Well, I know that you're very busy so first of all thanks for giving up your time.' Then I reiterate why I wanted to see them in the first place: 'I really wanted to learn more about the way you go about organizing training and development within the firm, as well as find out more about the organization other than what I've picked up from your website.'

Often the other person will ask you what you know about their business and it's then that you can mention some of the stuff you managed to glean in your preliminary research. Then your conversation should use some of the strategies I explain in the rest of this chapter, such as asking the right questions and focusing on features and benefits.

Asking Questions

I reckon anyone with half a brain knows about closed questions and open questions, so I won't insult your intelligence by telling you what you already know.

Similarly, it's often the case that a book such as this will group questions into categories: reflective questions, enquiry questions, questions designed to seek commitment and so on. I don't do that, because when you're in a sales meeting – unless you're sheep-like, insistent on following some kind of sales 'procedure' or schematic or cycle – then so long as you're asking relevant questions, it really doesn't matter in what order you ask them.

What I do strongly suggest you do, however, is consider the kind of questions you want to know the answers to prior to going into the meeting, and even write them down so that you don't forget. Once you get confident with these sorts of meetings, you'll find yourself asking roughly similar questions each time. However, as with small talk, it's the listening that's more important than the questions.

Of course, what you want to ask will be determined by what you hope to get from the meeting and then, as the meeting progresses, by the answers you receive to those questions.

Questions to Ask

It would be daft to try to list all the possible questions you could ask in such a meeting, but here are a few general ones, applicable no matter what you're selling:

- What/who do you use for this product/service at the moment?
- How did that relationship come about?
- What do you like about your current supplier?
- Is there anything you'd change about the service/product you currently receive/use? (This follows on from the previous

question, but it wouldn't be right to ask: 'What don't you like about them?' This is a more delicate way of finding out.)

- What is your annual spend on these products/this service?
- Who else is in your department?
- When will the supplier list be reviewed?
- Other than you, who else is involved in the decision of which supplier to use?
- What kind of relationship do you want with your suppliers?

Why Questions

Why is 'Why?' not included in the list of questions?

A 'why' question is best avoided if possible, because when you ask somebody why they chose to follow a particular course of action or made a decision, you are asking them to justify that decision. And when you do that you are immediately putting them on the defensive, which you want to avoid when attempting to influence and persuade them to use your services or products.

Once again, this is all about how you phrase things. Words are seriously important, in that the meaning you intended to convey may not be the meaning the receiver interprets. You must choose your words carefully to reflect the way your listener speaks. You'll only learn the answer to that if you really listen to them and pick up on the way they phrase things.

This whole area is known as psycholinguistics and forms much of the background to neurolinguistic programming (NLP). It's not something I profess to know a huge amount about, so if you want to learn more, read some of the many books on the subject or, even better, get my sister to teach you: go to www.rebeccainspires.com.

Let's look in more detail at a couple of the questions above. First, 'Other than you, who else is involved in the decision of which supplier to use?'

You need to find out who makes the decision *and* who signs off the money. They may be two different people and you need to know.

If you are sitting in front of the decision maker but not the person with the cash, you need to ask them, one, the name of that individual and two, whether they can arrange to meet up with them; the name of the M.A.N., in other words.

Let's say that Anya tells you that she's the decision maker but that she has to run costs by Holly. You need to ask – there and then – whether Holly is around and whether you can meet her. In addition, the relationship between you and Anya is, at that moment, *HOT*, so she's far more likely to be amenable to your request.

There's another reason for this too. You are always going to be the best person to sell what you are offering. Anya may love what you do, but with all the will in the world she cannot convey the same depth of knowledge, passion or enthusiasm for your product or service as you can; and if you're selling a service that's doubly true.

So the conversation might go like this:

> **YOU:** *Aside from you, Anya, is there anyone else involved in deciding which supplier to go with?*
>
> **ANYA:** *Well, I make the final decision but it's my boss, Holly, who has to approve the cost of anything I suggest.*
>
> **YOU:** *Great, at least that takes the pressure off you a bit, not having to worry about the pennies. It'd be really nice to get a chance to catch up with Holly and introduce myself, is she around today?*

This does require you to be assertive, but it needs asking – strike while the iron (or hotplate) is hot and all that.

Anya may say: 'Sure, I'll give her a ring and see if she can pop in.' In that case this is a massive buying sign, because if she didn't want to buy then she wouldn't waste her boss's time by suggesting she meet you.

She may also reply along these lines: 'She's not about at the moment and anyway she will go with my recommendation.' This may or may not be true, but accept it at face value and don't push further. Simply make a note of Holly's name and position, because she's going to become someone to try to meet, perhaps via a networking event.

Secondly, 'What kind of relationship do you ideally want from a supplier?' This is a very touchy-feely question and one that I suspect many people don't consider asking, yet it's important.

It is too easy to fall into the trap of thinking about your organization as some kind of dispensary, dishing out products or services, and that customers regard you in the same way. But it is important to appreciate that it is the people within organizations who deal with one another and that, as such, there exists a relationship.

I'm reminded of some years back when my wife Lisa and I were considering selling our house. We invited three estate agents to view our property and to find out what they would do for their fee.

Fairly obviously, the primary reason we wanted an agent was to sell our house. We wanted a good brochure, to know where they would promote the property – press ads, websites, board outside and so on – and, of course, how much they charged.

However, there was more to it than that. We wanted to feel as though the agent was working with us rather than simply for us. We wanted them to really understand our motives behind moving and what we were looking to move into, and to appreciate our personal circumstances regarding times when we would be available for viewing.

We hoped to find someone who was as enthusiastic about our home as we were, but also who would be proactive, keep us informed but without hassling us every day. On the other hand, we certainly didn't want to have to keep chasing them up to find out how things were progressing.

The point is, no one asked. Not one of the agents bothered to find out how Lisa and I would prefer to be dealt with. Each agent assumed that as long as they could assure us that they would sell our house, that was all that mattered.

The questions I have detailed above are simply there as a guide. You probably won't want to ask all of them because if you're listening properly, the answers you hear will prompt you to ask others that you may not have even considered asking.

As soon as I have asked the first question, I always ask the person whether they mind if I take notes. No one has ever replied 'Yes'.

Taking notes allows you to recall what you discussed at a later date, prompts you to ask other questions and is a very clear indication to your prospect that you are genuinely interested in what they are saying.

Listen to their answers and watch out for opportunities to ask for business, or at least to move the conversation towards getting business.

Buying Signs

It would be impossible for me to list all the many and varied ways in which a prospect may express an interest (often referred to as a 'buying sign' by sales people), but here are a few:

- What do you charge? (If they weren't interested in what you had, they wouldn't care what you charged.)
- Can you deliver in the mornings?
- Does it come in black?
- Do you ever speak at conferences?
- Have you ever done . . . ?
- Would you consider . . . ?
- Would you like to meet our head of . . . ?

All these are questions that would not ordinarily be asked if the prospect was not interested. So the conversation might go along the lines of:

> *'Tell me, do you offer negotiation skills training?'*
> *'Yes, why do you ask?'*

Or:

> *'Do you offer half-day or full-day courses?'*
> *'Both. Which format do you normally prefer? Why, do you have anything in mind?'*

Warning: There is a phenomenon in sales referred to as 'selling yourself in and selling yourself out'. It is a blight often visited on the less experienced.

What happens is that the person selling has explained all about her product, the client says 'Yes' or gives a more subtle buying sign, but rather than stopping and getting the order signed, the seller carries on explaining more about her service or product. Meanwhile, the prospect hears something she says in her additional spiel, which causes him to have second thoughts. When she does finally ask for the business, he says that he'd better think about it and, on reflection, have a word with the finance director.

Again, selling is about listening, not simply information gathering. Sales people are always moving the conversation forward, looking out for opportunities to close the deal (I'll talk about closing itself later).

Features and Benefits

This must be one of the first topics any budding sales person learns about: the difference between benefits and features.

At some point in this meeting you are going to need to tell your potential client about what it is you and your company do: what services you provide, the kind of organizations you currently work for and the kind of projects with which you are involved.

However, what you tell this person will be dictated by the information you have gleaned from the questions you asked.

Telling a prospect that you have offices throughout the UK is a complete waste of time if you know that they operate solely within the M25. On the other hand, if they have mentioned that they have plans to open another depot/branch/office in the North West, then letting them know that you've a place in Warrington would be a great idea.

You need to do this, as it lets them know that you have listened to what they've been saying.

The temptation to trot out a stream of facts about your firm, product or service is a strong one. Often this is delivered like an automated response and in a state of nervousness, as if you were an understudy delivering lines for the first time who just wants to get it over and done with:

- We are the largest provider of X in the UK.
- We have 12 offices in the UK.
- We deal with 50% of the FTSE 100 companies.
- We have 35 people in our CDR team.
- We are committed to total client care and provide bespoke commercial solutions to a range of high net worth clients, globally.

The final one is trite, meaningless rubbish, but it's the sort of drivel that one hears all too often.

Let's take the rest in turn.

- We are the largest provider of X in the UK.

Issues arising out of such a statement might include: Who says? By what do you measure that?

If you are going to say something along these lines, it sounds much more credible if you can support it in some way: 'According to independent research carried out by our industry's professional trade association, we are the largest provider of X in the UK.'

But so what? I'm not being flippant here, but what do I care that you are the biggest in the UK, even if you have just supported it with evidence? In fact, while you might think that being the biggest is great, I might be thinking: 'I don't want to deal with some huge, faceless organization. What I want is a smaller, more caring firm.' Or: 'You won't want my business in that case because I'm too small for you; you probably just deal with the big firms, don't you?'

- We have 12 offices in the UK; and We deal with 50% of the FTSE 100 companies.

Possible issues might include: 'You must be expensive then, because running 12 offices costs money, transport, lighting, heating, rent etc. and I don't want to be paying for that when I buy stuff from you. I've just got a place in Sevenoaks, so I need only deal with a firm in and around London.' Or: 'You will be too bureaucratic to deal with. It's easier just dealing with one office.'

- We have 35 people in our CDR team.

The response might be: 'I have no idea what CDR is but I don't wish to be seen as unintelligent by asking so I'll just nod.'

The vast majority of lawyers will know that CDR refers to commercial dispute resolution, the department that deals with breaches of contract, health and safety regulations and employment issues.

It's easy to use language with which you are familiar and to assume that everyone else knows what you're on about. Of course, you'll know whether you can use such specialist language if you have asked the right questions and listened to the answers, because you'll have found out the extent of the person's knowledge. Indeed, they may well have used technical, industry-specific language in their responses to you.

Other issues with this statement are: 'Is 35 a lot?' 'Does that make you a big player within CDR or a small one and anyway, so what?'

Simply mentioning a figure to someone who has little knowledge of your profession has no meaning to them and therefore has no impact or, worse, it conjures up a negative thought. They may think that 35 makes you a big player and therefore impersonal and expensive, or a small fish and not able to cope with more detailed stuff or to handle big orders.

Instead, look to sell the benefits:

- We have 35 people in our CDR department which means that you'll get a better service.
- We have 35 people in our CDR department so we are able to handle all your queries.
- We have 35 people in our CDR department, which means that you can deal with the person you feel most comfortable with.

Wants and Needs

Appreciating the difference between wants and needs is vital and will enable you to be more precise in your questioning and reveal your prospect's real needs.

Wants are expressed, whereas needs are the implicit desires and wishes that lie behind those explicit wants. An easy illustration explains the difference.

You are my boss and you are conducting my annual appraisal. It goes well. I'm enjoying my work and you've told me you think I'm doing a great job.

Towards the end of the appraisal you tell me that you are awarding me a £2000 pay increase.

'Oh,' say I, 'I wanted £6000.'

You tell me it's £2000 I'm getting, so I repeat the fact that I want £6000.

We argue, haggle and eventually agree on £4000.

You aren't happy, because that's £2000 more than you'd budgeted for and now you're going to have to award the other three members of the team the same or explain to them why you thought I deserved an extra £2000. On top of that, you're also going to have to justify the decision to your boss (no one makes decisions in isolation), all of which is a thorough pain in the neck.

At the same time, I'm annoyed and disgruntled because it is £2000 less than I wanted; I feel cheated.

In a situation such as this, there is only one way you can satisfy my demand for £6000 and that is to give it to me. That's what I want and that's the only way I will be satisfied.

What if, instead of accepting that demand ('wants' are demands), you acknowledged it but then asked me how I'd arrived at that figure and why I needed that kind of pay increase.

There may be loads of reasons why I need £6000:

- To pay off debt
- In order to pay for an operation for a relative
- School fees
- Baby on the way
- House extension
- Harry Potter first edition.

So listen intently. Your prospect will come right out and tell you what they want. Your job is to ask more questions, listen and uncover what lies behind those wants: what do they really need?

Once you know their needs, then you can go about addressing them.

When in recruitment, I once received an email from a relatively good client asking for a meeting to discuss a reduction in our fee. In fact, the email stated that unless I was prepared to reduce our fee from 20% of the first year's salary to 15%, there was no point in meeting because 15% was what he wanted.

I politely replied, saying that on this occasion we would not be prepared to drop to that level and that therefore I didn't wish to waste his time. And that was an end to the matter; or so I assumed.

However, three weeks later, Dave telephoned to ask me to come in for a meeting, although he was keen to stress that he still wanted the 15% rate.

We met and for 20 minutes Dave and the HR manager, who I did not know was going to be present, gave me the reasons why they wanted 15%.

'We want to reduce our costs.'

'We want you to do what another three agencies have done and reduce your fee to 15%.'

'We want you to know that we are firm on this and will not be moved.'

I nodded politely to all their concerns, but stuck to my original position of not reducing our fee. I reasserted why we charged what we did and reminded them of the strong relationship we had built up over the years and the very high level of service they received from us.

As the meeting went on, Dave began to relax and his demeanour became more amenable. He started to tell me about the changes that had taken place within the firm and that now he had to report directly to the Managing Partner, who was the kind of guy who wanted to be kept informed on a monthly basis of all expenditure, in contrast to the previous set-up, where Dave was pretty much his own boss.

That is when I realized what Dave 'needed': he needed to get his boss off his back. He needed to be able to show his boss that he was a dynamic practice manager who could control costs and screw suppliers down. He needed to be able to go back to his boss and show him that he had reduced recruitment costs.

By my sitting there and listening to Dave, allowing him to let off steam, he had finally revealed the real need behind his expressed 'want'. What is more, his telling me that three of his suppliers had already reduced their fees meant that he *could* go back to his boss saying he'd be saving money; just not from us.

However, I also pointed out something he had not thought about. Namely, if I received the CV of a lawyer in whom he might be interested, I'd naturally send that CV first to firms that would pay a 20% fee rather than 15% (unless the candidate in question had specifically asked to be forwarded to Dave's firm).

Listen to what people are really saying. Do not accept their expressed 'wants' at face value. Sit back, ask more questions and find out what 'needs' lie behind them. And then seek to address those.

CHAPTER 9

ASK

YOU'VE WOOED AND COURTED WITH – IT'S TIME TO GO FOR THE KISS

B efore you leave the meeting there's one thing you need to do . . . *ASK*. Ask for the business or the order.

You've targeted, you've connected, you've met – now it's time for the final step in the model.

Earlier on I said that following up after networking was the thing that the vast majority of people hate in the business development process. I lied.

It's asking that people hate the most; loathe and detest, even.

And whenever I ask people why they find this the most hated aspect, the answer is always that they fear rejection: that big fat, loud, all-consuming 'No'.

In this chapter we are going to look at how you should ask, when you should ask and why you should ask, as well as finding out how to deal with objections or concerns the prospect may raise and what to do when you hear the mind-numbingly non-committal and potentially soul destroying 'Leave it with me, I'll think about it'. Aargh!

First Things First: You Must ASK

Actually, to be completely accurate, ask and then say nothing.

That's it, folks. Sure, there are loads of books out there detailing bucketloads of closing techniques, from the exotic to the downright weird, from the 'order form close' through to the intriguingly titled 'Duke of Wellington', but these techniques all share one thing in common: they're rubbish.

Developing business is no different from trying to get someone into bed (more or less). No, seriously, bear with me on this one.

You fancy someone and think you'd like to develop a relationship with them. You have absolutely no way of knowing whether this person is going to be someone you'll simply share conversation with, or hold their hand, or kiss passionately, or sleep with, or even end up spending the rest of your life with. However, there is an attraction – at least on your part – so you figure that it's worth getting to know them.

Much in the same way, when you approach a stranger at a networking event you have no idea whether you are simply going to spend a very convivial 20 minutes chatting with them or they're going to end up being your best client ever and the person who makes you a fortune.

If you like the look of someone (we're back to dating here) then you have two choices:

- You walk right up to them and say 'Do you fancy coming to bed with me?'
- You start out on courting or wooing them (old-fashioned phrases but ones that everyone understands).

The first option is certainly more direct, cuts out any of the nonsense and gives you instant feedback – albeit a great deal of it may be negative. And, if you are thick-skinned enough, it might be the one you prefer. It's the one that companies selling replacement windows adopt when they phone you at home and try to sell you their wares, or the headhunter or independent financial adviser. No courtship, just straight to the point.

However, generally speaking that's not the way we go about developing a relationship in our society, whether of a business or romantic
nature.

Most non-sales people excel at the wooing and the courtship.
Not only do they appreciate that simply going up to prospective
customers and asking 'Do you fancy buying this or do you want
us provide this service?' is not the done thing, but neither would
they feel at all comfortable with being so direct. They understand
that bringing in new business takes time and involves a courtship
of sorts.

A romantic courtship runs something like this. We work in the same
building together, we catch each other's eye in the lift, and we exchange
a few words. We find out what department we work in and there's an
exchange of emails, which over time become a little flirty – but not
too much.

Things progress and soon we are meeting up for a coffee at lunchtime,
which becomes lunch. Maybe, after a couple of lunches together, I
suggest we grab something to eat one Saturday night.

So far so good. We are getting on, have found we have a lot in
common, share similar values, have talked about previous relationships and made it clear that we enjoy one another's company.

Dinner on a Saturday night is a world away from lunch during the
week. I know it; you know it. Neither of us has read a book that tells
us this. Our parents never sat us down and laid out the 'dating scale',
where coffee is at the bottom and dinner on a Saturday the top. We
just instinctively know.

Dinner works out great. There's a lot of flirting, the wine, the
food and the atmosphere help the mood and at the end of it there's
a kiss. Maybe not a full-blown snog yet, but a kiss nevertheless. If
we part without so much as a peck on the cheek, then it would
have turned out to be a disappointing night, because we had
expectations.

Following dinner and over the next few days or weeks we go to the theatre, take a walk in the park, go to the cinema and wander round a gallery.

A business courtship is very similar, but rather than the goal being to roll around in bed, it's securing a sale: both mutually satisfying (most of the time) but in a different way.

Prospective clients are taken for coffee then out to lunch with a view to establishing a stronger personal relationship and to learn more about them and how your product or service can be of benefit.

The client is then invited to the rugby or for a golfing day or perhaps to Glyndebourne or the Grand National, or maybe to the opening of a new art exhibition. All of that is courtship and a form of wooing.

But don't be under the mistaken belief that if you take your prospective business partner out for sufficient lunches, dinners and events then, by way of osmosis, you will just be given the business. It doesn't work like that.

Similarly, a prospective partner doesn't say to themselves: 'Oh well, I've been taken to The Ivy, then that preview of the latest exhibition at the Tate and they always order a Venti rather than a tall latte, so I might as well sleep with them.' At some point during a romantic courtship someone has to go for the kiss. You have to move in close and go for it. Otherwise there's a never-ending courtship, with both parties becoming increasingly confused about precisely what the other seeks from this 'relationship'. Are you going to end up in bed or be just good friends?

As a person in business you can wine and dine your prospective clients as much as you wish, but there comes a point where you have to do the business equivalent of going for the kiss – ask for their business. And you do this for the same reason as you would in a potentially romantic relationship. You cannot afford to be spending time courting someone who takes your hospitality but gives their business to a rival.

Sure, keep in touch, don't let them off your radar, but if they are happy with their current supplier, one sure way of learning that is asking them to do business with you. At that point they will let you know unequivocally that they intend to remain faithful – at least for the time being. And here is where business relationships do differ from romantic ones. A business relationship is never for life: organizations do change suppliers and neither are they monogamous – they are quite often up for a bit on the side so they can sample what else is out there and ditch who they have right now, should they ever feel taken for granted.

A few months back I was having a chat with the CEO of a law firm in the Midlands. He told me that a major PLC had been wooing and courting him over the previous two years. As part of this courtship he and his wife had been guests of the organization at the Cheltenham Festival – twice. They'd been taken to London to have a grandstand view of the London Marathon, which was followed by a cookery lesson given by a leading chef, topped off with a slap-up meal at said chef's restaurant.

When I commented on how lucky he was to have such corporate entertainment lavished on him, he paused and said: 'Yes, but do you know what, no one from the organization has yet approached me and asked for my business. To be honest, I haven't a clue what it is they want exactly.'

The prospect is expecting you to ask. If you start asking for the order every time you see people, I guarantee that your business development figures will go through the roof.

The Use of Silence

You might ask for the business something like this:

- So, it's been great having a coffee and learning about your business. Of course we'd love to do work for you. How do we go about doing that?

- I'm sorry to hear that you're no longer getting the service you once had with your current supplier. I'd love to help you out there. What can I do for you?

- The feedback from the last session was really good. I'd love to do more work with you, what else can I help you with?

- OK, I think last year went well and I know your purchasing manager was pleased with the price and delivery timescales. What orders do you think you'll be placing this year?

- Well, Harry, I have heard and understood what you've had to say about using an alternative/new supplier and I know that you appreciate that what we do could be of use/help to you. Obviously we'd love to supply these for you. What's the best way of getting to be considered?

- So you say you are looking at changing providers or at least reviewing the situation in May. Of course we'd love to be considered for that work/contract, when do we need to make our formal submission?

And so on. The point is: *ASK*. It may be trite but if you don't ask, the answer is always 'No'. If you don't ask, your competitors will.

But once you have asked, once you have posed a question similar to any of the above, *you must stop talking*.

Silence is the single most powerful way to close. People don't like silences, they're awkward, so when there is one we are tempted to fill it. That's fine when you have just asked for the business, just as long as it's not you who fills it! Shut up, look your prospect in the eye and wait.

Keep On Asking

It's not just prospective clients you need to ask for business, it's existing ones too. For example, Sean is the managing partner of a law firm with which I have had an association for nine years and I've known him for the past eight. When in the recruitment sector I did quite a bit of work with them, but training has been just now and again.

I had been thinking about approaching managing partners of small to mid-sized law firms directly, rather than going the normal route via the individuals charged with looking after their learning and development. I had never attempted this before, but given the economic climate I figured that a lot of them would be sitting at their desks wondering how they were going to generate more business and looking for 'quick wins'. In a training situation this would mean punchy, to-the-point sessions that would furnish senior lawyers with tools and advice they could put in to practice right away, rather than long-winded training programmes spread over months.

I confess that I tried this idea out on Sean, despite the fact that we had not spoken to one another for 18 months or so as I had been dealing with the HR manager. The email I sent him went like this:

> *Good morning Sean*
>
> *I was happily minding my own business when a copy of your in-house magazine landed on my door mat. Having devoured the contents I then noticed that for some reason they allow you to write the introduction!*
>
> *Anyway, I am delivering some training at Bond Academy on Friday afternoon, but wondered if you were free, and if you fancy a coffee and natter in the morning?*
>
> *Appreciate it's short notice, so no worries if you can't make it but thought it was worth asking.*
>
> *Nick*

He replied, letting me know that he wasn't free. So I sent this:

> *Let me run this by you, Sean. I'm doing a lot of BD/ selling training with partners at firms throughout the UK. Two formats:*

1 *Half-day intensive course on the essentials about following up leads, making appointments and closing business. Second half of the day: 45-minute one-to-one coaching sessions with those who attended to discuss strategies to help them achieve their specific BD goals.*

2 *I sit in a room from 9 until 5.30 and run a BD/selling surgery, with partners coming to chat to me about whatever problems, issues, difficulties they are having regarding bringing in more work.*

Cost: £X + VAT. No expenses and no preparation time. That's it. I'm doing this with several partnerships and they flippin' love it, plus your partners are made to feel as though you are really giving the support and tools necessary to win business in a difficult climate.

Let me know what you think and if you reckon it or a hybrid of it might be just the ticket.

Have fun.

Nick

What happened?

A day later the HR director got in touch and told me to pop in to meet her and a colleague. A few weeks later I was doing a day's training for all the partners.

Keep in touch. If you are visiting people in one area then go and see others in the same area, particularly existing clients. It lets them know that you still love them and that you are busy!

And keep asking for work. Just because they have bought from you in the past, don't get complacent and assume that if they want you they will get in touch. Come up with new ways of packaging or presenting what you offer.

Dealing with Objections

Asking for the business is also the only way you'll bring objections to the fore. And you need to know what your prospect's objections are if the relationship is to move from being about catching up every six months and enjoying one another's company, to trading with one another.

Objections are the reasons prospects will give you for not buying. They are like blockages in a pipe or a fallen tree across a road: they are in the way of your desired destination.

When you first hear an objection it's tempting to become defensive or get disheartened and pretend it doesn't matter. First things first: when it comes to objections, if you are getting them it's because your prospect doesn't understand the value of what it is you have to offer. In other words, you haven't done your job properly.

You know those really posh jewellers that have gorgeous things in the window with no price? They don't need price tags. You know that the shop is really expensive because of the overall impression that it gives you: the fixtures and fittings, the way the merchandise is displayed, the dress, appearance and demeanour of the staff, they way in which they approach and talk to you, the lighting, the flooring, the entire experience. In other words, if you do end up asking the price of a particular item, you are unlikely to express surprise at the cost. The retailer has handled the objection before it's even been raised by conveying a very strong message of luxury.

If you are in the business of selling a product, one that you can show to a prospective client, although they have something to see and touch they still might not appreciate the difference in quality between your offering and a competitor's, so you have to explain this.

The position is trickier if you are selling a service, because now it's completely down to you to bring your service to life and ensure that prospects know what they are getting for their money and what makes you a better choice.

Remember, when it comes to handling objections, prevention is better than cure. Know the strengths and weaknesses of your product. Be aware of the possible objections you may expect to hear and address them before a prospect brings them up.

Say that your firm has an office in London and one in Birmingham. Previous prospects have said that they worry you don't have other offices around the UK or one near where they are based. Rather than waiting for this to be raised or not mentioning it in the hope that they don't, during your meeting with a prospect make a point of telling them about customers you already have that are far from Birmingham and London.

Another approach might be to say:

> *Of course, because we don't have offices all over the UK, our operation is much more streamlined, which means our customers can get hold of us easily and are not paying for a large distribution network.*

Or:

> *The fact that we have offices in London and Birmingham enables us to get to all our clients across the country quickly and easily, which is something they tell us they appreciate.*

These phrases seek to knock any possible objection about location on the head even before the prospect has mentioned it.

What to Do If Objections Come Up

Don't be scared of objections, but don't take them at face value and simply counter them with a quick but polite reply. Instead, acknowledge the objection, discover more about why the issue has been raised, what's worrying the prospect – and then deal with it.

An objection might be phrased like this:

> **TIFFANY:** *Well, Ted, what you say sounds great and on principle I am happy to use your services. However, I'm a little concerned that you are more expensive than the other quotes I've received.*

The first thing to note here is that Ted has been thorough in his questioning, so he would know that she had obtained other quotes and – if she'd been willing to tell him – from which of his competitors. With his knowledge of the market, he should be aware roughly how much they would be charging.

So, when faced with the 'It's too expensive' objection, Ted should avoid the temptation to contradict:

> **TED:** *We like to think that our price reflects the current market rate.*

Or:

> *TED: Well, our research tells us that we are competitively priced.*

You wouldn't expect Tiffany's reply to be

> **TIFFANY:** *Oh well then, in that case I will buy.*

Here's what Ted should do. First, acknowledge the objection:

> **TED:** *'OK, price is a concern for you.'*

He should then write this down. Writing it down lets Tiffany know that he takes her concern seriously. Then he should add:

TED: *Is there anything else that concerns you about using us?*

Here he is being very up front. He might be scared to ask this, because what if Tiffany trots out an entire list of reasons? Well, what if she does? At least he'll know what hurdles he needs to get over.

If you go for the kiss and the person rejects you, then it'd be nice to know why, wouldn't it? If it's because they just see you as a friend, then there's not a lot you can do. If it's because your breath smells of garlic, then you can go to Boots, get some breath freshener and bingo: game on!

So don't be afraid to ask if there's anything else and get everything out in the open.

TIFFANY: *Yes, I'm a little concerned that you don't have a presence in the north east.*

TED: *OK. (He writes the objection down.) Anything else?*

TIFFANY: *No.*

TED: *Are you sure?*

TIFFANY: *Yes, that's all.*

TED: *OK, if I can assure you about these two things, would you feel comfortable to go ahead?*

That last is a cracking line and sorts the pros from the amateurs in developing business. What Ted has done here is use an objection as an opportunity to close.

This is sales ballet – elegant, yet powerful – and it moves him closer to a sale because he now knows that all he has to do is address those two concerns and Tiffany has told him she'll buy from him.

Let's just take one of the concerns: geographical location. Tiffany has let him know that she is concerned about the lack of an office in the North East.

The secret here is for Ted to discover what lies behind the objection. Often you'll find that a stated objection simply masks the real issue, and it is that which he must discover.

Reasons why Tiffany might have said this include:

- She can't be bothered travelling to his Birmingham office from where she lives in Sunderland.
- She's not the decision maker.
- She's worried that an engineer won't get to her quickly enough if there's a fault.
- She prefers to see the offices of the organizations with which she deals.
- She's concerned it'll cost more to get stuff to her.
- She's afraid she won't get the service levels she needs.
- There's an alternative supplier in Middlesbrough.
- She's attempting to reduce her carbon footprint and source things locally.
- She doesn't like Birmingham or London.

I could go on, but I'm sure you get the point.

In order to find out what the real worry is, Ted needs to ask:

TED: *So what is it in particular about the absence of an office in the North East that concerns you?*

If it's about levels of service, then he should deal with that and provide reassurance: mention the names of other organizations with which he deals that have offices a similar distance away, and so on with whatever the concern is.

The Really Awkward One
'I'll think about it.'

This isn't really an objection: it's not as definite as an objection, which is why people feel so deflated whenever they hear it. At least with a proper objection you can get to the reason behind it, but this is tricky.

First of all, as with any objection, ask:

> **YOU:** *What is there in particular that you feel needs further thought? I'm concerned that I have perhaps omitted to tell you something about our service/product that gives you the full picture.*
>
> **THEM:** *No, you've been very helpful and I feel I know everything I need to know. It's just that I like to give such matters some thought.*

Don't push here! If you start to get too pushy, you're going to annoy them and all that work you've done to get to know them will have been wasted. We all want to have time to think about purchasing decisions, so allow it.

Still, you want to keep control and not simply leave them with the ball in their court. That being the case, here's what you say.

> **YOU:** *Fine, of course you want to think about it and I don't want to hassle you, so I'll leave it with you. If I've not heard from you within 2-3 weeks/3-6 months, when shall I drop you a line to see where we're up to?*

I did this recently at the end of a very convivial meeting. The prospect said she wanted to think about things and that first she had to persuade the management team that soft skills training was important. I told her that I would leave it with her and that I wouldn't bother her again (people appreciate this, because most people set on business development do pester), but asked when I should next get in touch. I then gave her two options (the alternative close): 'In a couple of months or in the New Year?' to which she replied: 'Give me a call in January.'

We both knew where we stood and I had her permission to get in touch in January. She knew that I would not bother her and equally I wasn't left wondering whether, over the following few months, I could get in touch or leave it a little longer, which freed me up to concentrate on other potential clients for whom the timing might be better.

I had another client with whom I did loads of work and the feedback was great. We then lost touch for a year (I left one firm and set up on my own), but a chance meeting on a train with one of the senior directors resulted in another piece of work, which I duly delivered. Then I was asked to quote for work right at the last minute, which I did but did not win.

As part of my continual keeping in touch and going to see clients, I visited the head of training and her assistant. The meeting went well; we always have a laugh together. However, I asked them if there was anything else I could help them with and there was a pause, which told me that there was a problem: a blockage to business.

So I asked them to tell me what was on their mind and they did. They were worried that I only did 'one thing':

> **CLIENT:** *I have seen you deliver training, Nick, and I'm worried that what I saw is all you do. It was very good, but only for those kinds of big audience gigs.*
> **ME:** *OK, what worries you about that?*

She expanded and I made a note and listened intently.

I then reminded her of all the other stuff I had done for the firm in the past that was to groups of six to eight and had been on different topics. I also mentioned – referring to the names of clients she would recognize – other training sessions I had delivered and the response I'd had.

> **ME:** *Is there anything else?*

> **CLIENT:** *Yes, when I called you to ask you to quote for that bit of work some months back, I asked another provider as well and whereas they came to see me because they felt they needed to know more before putting a proposal together, you didn't. You just sent something over in writing.*
>
> **ME:** *That's true. Can I ask you what bothered you about that?*

She told me that she felt that in my eagerness to secure the work, I had simply cobbled something together and that, in contrast to the other provider, she felt I had not put a lot of thought into it.

I mentioned the fact that when she had asked me to quote and provide a training outline, she had said she needed it urgently, which was why I hadn't requested a meeting to find out more about her requirements. Ordinarily I would, and in fact that's the way I prefer to work.

So, with everything out in the open, we were able to talk through her worries and I was able to address them. I thanked her for being so honest and was glad that she felt she could bring this to my attention.

What is amazing is that the two of them went on to say that the only reason they felt comfortable expressing their views was the fantastic relationship we had together. What is more – and this is the whole point of this – they told me that normally they don't bother telling suppliers why they won't use them.

Shortly after, I was asked to quote on some work and now all is back on track with the relationship.

Feel, Felt, Found

I was taught the three words *FEEL*, *FELT* and *FOUND* back in 1988 and they are as good today as they were then. Let me give you an example:

PROSPECT: *I'm worried that you don't have an office in the North East.*

YOU: *I know exactly how you* **FEEL.** *To be honest, you won't be surprised to hear that a number of our clients* **FELT** *exactly the same way before using us, but what they have since* **FOUND** *is that they get either the same or a better level of service than they did before, because with only two offices internal communication is so much more joined up.*

Possible Outcomes

To summarize: when you receive an objection, acknowledge it. Find out what lies behind it — the real reason — and then address it. Do this with each one in turn and check with the prospect whether they are comforted by your answer. If they're not, find out what is still bothering them and repeat the process.

At the end of the meeting, with all objections dealt with, there are a number of possible outcomes:

1. They love you and your product and want to do business with you.
2. They love you and your product, but want to think about it/ have a word with a colleague.
3. They love you and your product, but are happy with their current supplier.
4. They love you, but aren't keen on what you're offering.
5. They don't like you one little bit.

There must be loads of other possible outcomes, but I reckon that these five cover 99% of them. Here's what you do in each case:

1. Great – get the ball rolling/order form signed/delivery date agreed.

2. No problem. If you have asked the right questions, then you'll know who the colleague is and you'll have already asked how you go about setting up a meeting with them. If it's someone you don't know or meeting them isn't possible, then tell your contact that you will leave it with them, but check when you should get in touch if you don't hear from them in 2–3 weeks (use the alternative close and make sure that they see you make a note of the date in your diary).

3. Fine. If you have asked the right questions, you'll know when the decision's up for review and have asked them when you should next be in touch, because 'I'd love to be considered for that'. Even if that's not an option – they aren't reviewing it in the foreseeable future – let them know that you won't bother them but will perhaps drop them a line to see if your timing's better.

4. Acknowledge the fact that you can't help them. If you feel comfortable, ask if they know anyone who would be interested in what you have, or ask them what they would be interested in buying and, if possible, start supplying it – if the set-up cost is not too high and/or you think existing customers might want it.

5. Shake their hand. Thank them for their time and when you're far enough away, mutter 'NEXT!' under your breath.

EPILOGUE

I am often asked whether I think sales people are born, whether it's a natural talent that can't really be learned.

My view is this. Around 10% of people in any organization are the technical whizz-kids. Often known as 'nerds' or 'techies', these are the experts in their field. They understand all the detail, love the minutiae of things and will produce the most detailed reports, covering all the bases. However, they are not terribly comfortable with human interaction. Every firm has them and although they drive us mad sometimes, we couldn't do without them.

Another 10% are the 'born' sales people. These are the wheeler-dealers in the playground, through college and university (if they bother going). Selling is what they do and who they are. Lovely, affable and chatty, their optimism and 'the next big deal' are what drive them on. We love them, but often in only small doses and we can't understand how they live so close to the edge income-wise.

Then there are the rest of us: the 80%. We are neither of the other two, although there's a bit of each in all of us, just toned down.

I'm one of those but with one difference: I was taught how to sell. I was taught and coached by Mark Brundrett and John Mifflin, in my first proper job as a 21-year-old sales rep and then again in my next sales job, where I was sent on courses. I had also been taught while at Russell & Bromley, both as a 17-year-old part-time, weekend/ holiday member of staff and then again as a full-time employee while studying for my degree.

In all these roles I was taught the theory and then had the opportunity to put it in to practice – years and now decades of practice and thousands upon thousands of customers. And that's the difference, practice.

If you've been reading this book, the chances are that you're not 'in sales' and certainly don't regard yourself as a 'salesperson'. You're not going to be as good as the person with loads of experience under their belt and neither do you want to be doing that much selling; if you did, you'd have gone into sales rather than the role you are in at the moment.

But you can get better. You can become more proficient. Read some books. Learn from people like me who have cocked it up and nearly gone bankrupt so that you don't make the same errors. Understand how to work smart at developing business, rather than hard.

Try some of the ideas and tips I've given you. If they work for you: great. If not, try again and if they still don't: NEXT!

But above all, be yourself. Don't be seduced by the idea that you have to be earnest and business-like in order to come across as competent and professional when going out to develop some business.

And you don't need to know it all before you start. In fact, I read recently that when people make mistakes we are more persuaded by them than we are by those who are 'perfect'. When people show their vulnerability we warm to them because they appear human; like us. Those of you who saw Levi Roots doing his pitch on *Dragon's Den* a few years ago will know what I mean.

Have a Style

You can't have got this far and not realized that it is ultimately *you* that people buy, not your product or service. Given that that is the case, it is essential that you reflect your personality when you *CONNECT* and *MEET* with people.

I have furnished you with loads of examples of my own character and style. In fact, you should have been able to get a very good sense of that even if I hadn't bothered including example letters and emails: the book should speak loudly enough in the way it is written, which is, of course, what I wanted.

Being 'you', being authentic, should be the easiest thing in the world, but when put in 'work mode' we all tend to wear a mask. While you cannot behave in the world of work as you do with your mates or at home, if you are to have success in developing business, then you must allow people to see you minus the disguise.

For some of you it'll take a while until you feel comfortable with this idea; for others it'll be a blessed relief to ditch that fake persona you've been under the impression you had to adopt.

You must develop your own style, though. You aren't Nick Davies and I'm not you.

Keep Doing It

Winning work and developing business and selling never stop. Even when you are slammed busy you must never, ever stop.

An email, a letter, a phone call, a cup of coffee or tea with someone – it doesn't matter what it is, but you *must* do at least one thing every day to move your business forward.

There is only one exception to this rule and that's if you are starting from scratch, either establishing a new department/team or beginning your own business. In these cases you have only one option and that is to take **massive action**. You're going to have to make calls, write letters and fire off emails like your life depended on it... because it does, your commercial/financial life at least.

Pick 'n' Mix

I'm going to leave you with an assortment of thoughts and things to consider when developing business is part of your job or you're thinking about going out on your own.

For People Running or Considering Running Their Own Business

- Do something you enjoy.
- Make sure that you can make money from it.
- Keep overheads low.
- Don't listen to sheep (you know who they are).
- When you stop enjoying it, stop doing it.
- You will make less money than you think.
- The vast majority of business forecasts and cash flow projections are crap and are there simply to make the bank happy. They provide you with a modicum of comfort, but are as useful as birthing plans: out the window as soon as the hard work starts!
- If you have to do a forecast then be pessimistic – and then halve it.
- You can charge more than you think for your product or service.
- Offer discounts, but don't say 'yes' to any price just because it makes you feel as though you are making progress. If you sell too cheap then it's really hard to charge that same customer

more next time round: they don't value your product as much as they did and other people will want the same, cheap rate. Be proud of your price.

- Don't say 'yes' to every order that comes in – even though you'll really, really want to.

For Employed People Who Have to Develop Business alongside Their Primary Role

- If you aren't enthusiastic or don't think you could be given the right training, then let someone else do it. You'll never be great at it because your heart won't be in it.

- If you don't believe in what you are selling or promoting, then don't bother.

- You are going to need to get the input and cooperation of others within the business, so get good at making friends.

- If you're not working on a commission or bonus basis get that changed: you'll want to be rewarded for your success.

- You need to set aside business development time every single day – even if it's simply sending one email or one letter or making one phone call or having a coffee with a potential or existing client. (If you don't do something each day then you should feel bad about it and lose sleep.)

- If you and your team are tasked with winning more work, you need to have a weekly meeting. Make this quick, punchy and to the point – just enough time to find out what you're all doing in the week ahead and what you've got on the go. This builds camaraderie and ensures that you're leaving no opportunity to fall through the gaps.

- When connecting with potential clients, don't upset the pow-ers-that-be by deviating too much from the house style, but do make sure that as much of your personality comes across as possible.

- Leave if your firm doesn't understand the importance of setting time aside for developing business. Any organization in this day and age that hasn't grasped just how important going out and winning work is deserves to go under. Make sure that you're not on board when it does.

Sales people like selling because it affords them a huge amount of autonomy and they can earn an indecent amount of money. However, they don't do it for the money – not those who stick at it. They do it for the thrill. They do it for that moment when the man or woman in front of them says 'Yes' – a man or woman who maybe only a few months back had never heard of them or their product, but who now has such faith in the relationship that the sales person has established, cultivated and nurtured that they are happy to buy what they are offering.

And I can tell you, that doesn't matter if it's a jar of shoe polish, a multithousand-pound training contract or even a book deal: the feeling is just the same.

Hopefully what I have shared with you will help you experience this euphoria and although you don't ever want to be regarded as a sales person, you will at least be on your way to being great at something you used to hate.

Good luck.

Nick

ACKNOWLEDGEMENTS

It's customary to make acknowledgments in a book and so, not wishing to fly in the face of convention, here are mine. They're a tad gushing and emotional in places, but it's my book, so tough.

My first thanks go to Mark Brundrett and John Mifflin. I don't know whether they are still about, since I have tried looking for them on the usual sites but can't find them. Mark was my first sales manager at Reed International and John was the bloke in whose classroom I sat at head office in East Grinstead for two weeks in late 1987 being taught how to sell ad space. Thank you to both of you for your enthusiasm and passion and for giving me the foundation on which my entire working life has been built.

Mum: Two kids, a single parent with an O level in cookery, living in a terraced house with a backyard in a suburb of north Manchester. Trips to the launderette on a Friday with our washing in a Tesco trolley, free school meals. Yet you put yourself through college, then polytechnic and after years of hard work typing night after night into the early hours at the desk in your bedroom, you qualified as a teacher and eventually became head of year. I can think of no better role model for having a goal, sticking to it and persisting despite the odds. You were the first person to read the first draft of the manuscript of this book and cast your former English teacher eye over it (and you hadn't lost your touch with the red pen!). Thank you.

Dad: Selling was in your blood from being a rep in your twenties, flogging Angel Delight and Maxwell House coffee for General Foods, to running your own promotions agency to promoting your driving instructor skills today. Selling and marketing are what you've always done and had a passion for. Your love of business, of doing the deal and of living life to the full, always being positive, is what you've passed on to me. Thank you.

Sue and Andy Groocock (odd name, great people). These good friends live in what must be the remotest part of mainland UK, a house outside of the busy, heaving metropolis that is Applecross. In February 2010 I spent a week at their B&B, www.spindrift-applecross.co.uk, hunched over my laptop, typing the vast majority of this book. I should have only been there for two nights but was snowed in and had to stay for the week. Sue baked and cooked and generally looked after me through the cold days, but left me alone to get this done. Thank you.

Bren Tierney and John Hyslop, friends for as long as I can remember and two of the best sales people you'll ever meet. Neither has a degree, they just started in sales at the bottom and worked their way up, doing what sales people do: making the calls, visiting the customer, asking for the order and hitting their target. Thank you.

Patrick McCann, friend and Global Head of Learning and Development at Herbert Smith. Patrick gave me my first break into the world of training members of the legal profession when he was head of learning and development at Berwin Leighton Paisner. He has been and remains my biggest advocate for what I do and the way I deliver it. Thank you.

Vincent Connor, Partner and Head of Asia Pacific and Head of the Hong Kong office of Pinsent Masons, a good business acquaintance and the best networker and worker of a room I have ever witnessed. Vincent is the very epitome of a polite, affable, immaculately tailored, erudite Edinburgh gentleman lawyer. Thank you for allowing me to hold you up as an example in virtually every course on networking I run.

Simon Shaw, a fellow Mancunian now living in Edinburgh and a superb graphic designer. He's the guy responsible for designing the booklets I hand out at the end of sessions and the success that they are. People love the look and feel of them and that's all down to him. Thank you for helping me to be remembered.

Iain Campbell, Jenny, Grace, Louise, Megan, Laura & Emily at Wiley/Capstone. From our first meeting at Costa on Victoria train station in London right through to the publication of this book, Iain has been with me every step of the way. He has been a fantastic advocate for me and this book and there's no way any of it would have happened without him. Jenny read and re-read the manuscript and made sure the whole thing flowed and made sense.

Roy Dobbs, my friend and my former boss at Russell & Bromley in Manchester. The finest retailer you'd ever wish to meet. Roy has more passion and flair for retail than anyone I've met. He taught me that sales is not simply about product knowledge, it's about delivering a performance, putting on a show; that the customer should be entertained and leave having had a retail 'experience'.

My wife, Lisa. She has stuck with me since our first date on 22 September 1989, through a business failure, near bankruptcy, a law degree, Bar school, eight house moves, including one from Manchester to Edinburgh with a 14-month-old son, two new business start-ups and a handful of career changes, all the whilst being a senior account manager, training to be a beauty therapist and bringing up our two boys, George and Harry. Your love and support and unerring faith in me allowed me to get to this point. I simply could not have done it without you. I love you. Thank you.

Rebecca, my sister. For putting up with me tormenting her when we were growing up, for persuading me to start a recruitment business with her and for believing in me when many didn't. Thank you.

ABOUT THE AUTHOR

Nick Davies LLB (hons) barrister

Hi, I'm Nick Davies. I'm a tall Mancunian, Blue Peter badge winner and the bloke who owns 'The Really Great Training Company.'

My background's in law and business. I've been a sales rep, a sandwich maker, and even sold shoes for Russell & Bromley for 6 years – where David Beckham and Vera Duckworth were customers. I've also been the director responsible for business development at two limited companies, and started 4 businesses of my own. I qualified as a barrister as a mature student and even practised . . . for 6 months (the wig just wasn't me.)

As a trainer and coach in a range of communication skills, I travel the country, teaching bankers, lawyers, actuaries, civil servants and business people how to pitch, present, network, sell and persuade.

My clients range from global legal practices and financial institutions to small, owner-managed firms as well as The Royal Household (a kind of more grand owner-managed firm.)

When I'm not training and coaching I perform stand-up, deliver after-dinner speeches and host award ceremonies. Over the past few years I've been lucky enough to have worked and shared stages with a buffet of reasonably well-known people; including: The Rt. Hon. Michael Portillo, Sir Digby Jones, Jenny Bond, Kate Adie, Roger Black MBE, Max Clifford, Alan Hansen, Frankie Boyle and Alastair Campbell.

INDEX

INDEX